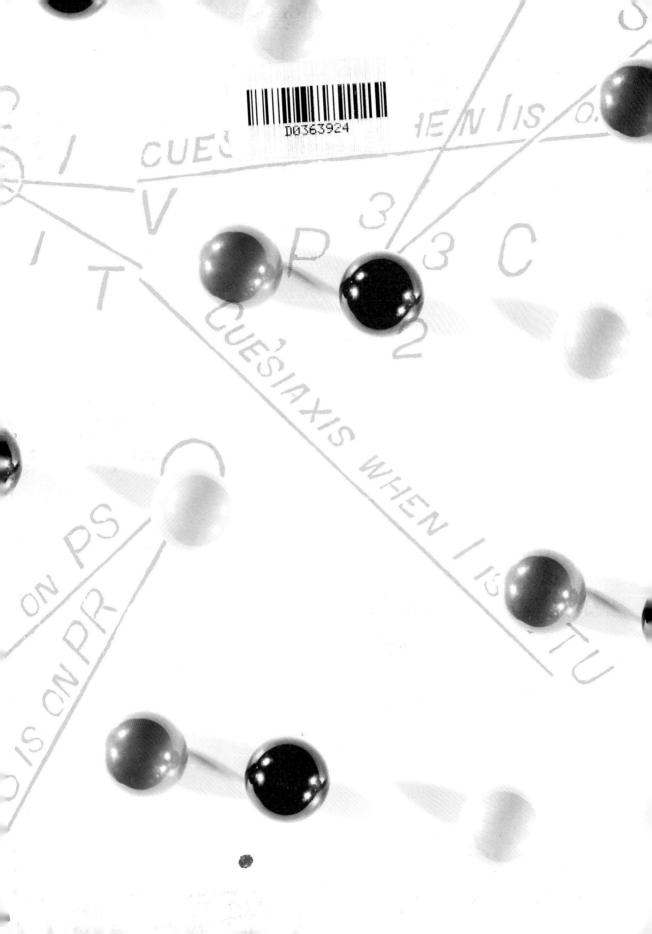

THE BOOK OF
OF
SNOOKER
DISASTERS
&
BIZARRE
RECORDS

Also available
**The Cricketer Book of
Cricket Disasters and Bizarre Records**
Christopher Martin-Jenkins
**The Cricketer Book of
Cricket Eccentrics and Eccentric Behaviour**
Christopher Martin-Jenkins
**The Book of Rugby
Disasters and Bizarre Records**
Fran Cotton
**The Book of Golf
Disasters and Bizarre Records**
Chris Plumridge
Bedside Darts
Sid Waddell

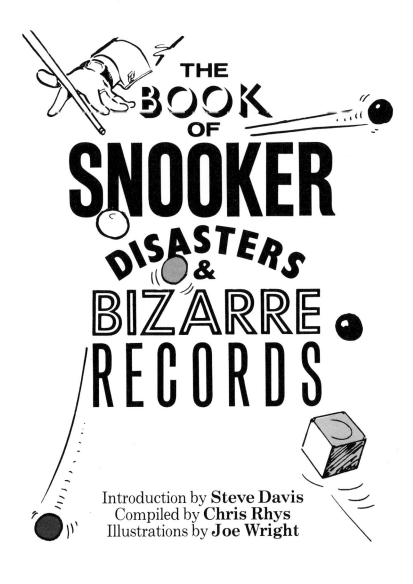

THE BOOK OF SNOOKER DISASTERS & BIZARRE RECORDS

Introduction by **Steve Davis**
Compiled by **Chris Rhys**
Illustrations by **Joe Wright**

Stanley Paul
London Melbourne Auckland Johannesburg

Stanley Paul & Co. Ltd

An Imprint of Century Hutchinson Ltd
62-65 Chandos Place, London WC2N 4NW

Century Hutchinson (Australia) Pty Ltd
16-22 Church Street, Hawthorn, Melbourne,
Victoria 3122

Century Hutchinson (NZ) Ltd
32-34 View Road, Glenfield, Auckland 10

Century Hutchinson (SA) Pty Ltd
PO Box 337, Bergvlei 2012, South Africa

First published 1986

Set in Century Schoolbook

Made by Lennard Books
Mackerye End, Harpenden
Herts AL5 5DR

Editor Michael Leitch
Designed by David Pocknell's Company Ltd
Production Reynolds Clark Associates Ltd
Printed in Great Britain by Butler & Tanner Ltd, Frome and London

British Library Cataloguing in Publication Data
Rhys, Chris
The book of snooker disasters and bizarre records.
1. Snooker – Anecdotes, facetiae, satire, etc.
I. Title
794.7'35'0207 GV900.S6

ISBN 0 09 166000 9

CONTENTS

INTRODUCTION

On the whole we snooker players have a pretty reasonable sense of humour, despite the fact that we may look desperately serious when we are at the table. I can think of few players who really object to being the centre of a joke. One who actually plays on it is the game's very own Count Dracula.

I got a lot of stick over being featured on TV's *Spitting Image* programme, but the truth of it is I was so delighted I kept it on video and still have a good laugh at myself. I really am very proud of the puppet and to be honest it looks better than the real thing; certainly more interesting. I haven't found out yet whether it plays snooker better!

That really is the key to it all – being able to share a laugh at yourself as well as at others. No one does this better than Dennis Taylor, which isn't bad when you think there must have been more jokes about his glasses than the mother-in-law. Naturally form does help you take the odd jibe better; there's nothing worse than having to sit there smiling sweetly when your snooker world is falling around your ears.

Some players find it a lot easier to show different reactions when playing, without necessarily breaking their concentration. What has to be realized, however, is that when you're on the table you must take yourself and the situation seriously. Off the table it's a different matter.

John Virgo is a great comic and has deservedly earned a reputation for his take-offs (of players, that is!). But deep down John would far rather be world champion. On the table, he can be one of the most miserable looking players – yet he's the funniest off it.

To a degree, Cliff Thorburn and Terry Griffiths are the same: very funny people away from the cloth, but deadly serious in a match. On the other side, Fred Davis had the knack of keeping a permanent smile on his face, even in adversity.

One aspect of being a snooker player that I will always be grateful for is that something is always happening, whether disastrous, bizarre or just highly amusing. And when the dividing line between these is so narrow, you have to be ready to accept whatever comes and if necessary extract as much humour from the situation as you can.

MR COURTNEY THE AMATEUR BILLIARD CHAMPION

MR GASKELL

MR FAY

THE COMMON BILLIARD SPECTATOR

I have to look back at the crash I had in my Porsche when I came pretty close to total disaster. Thank you, seat belts! When we crashed, I had won four cases of whisky with the highest break for four rounds on the trot at the Jameson's. All, I hasten to add, were still unopened.

When I got out of the car, I noticed that one of the cases had dropped right on top of my cue case and buckled it. My only reaction was 'God, my cue's broken!' For those who don't know or play the game, losing your cue is worse than losing an arm.

I had even ignored my driver who was screaming at me: 'Steve, I can't get out!' It sounds terrible, but I just had to open that case before looking after him.

Both, fortunately, survived. Incidentally, for any souvenir hunter reading this, there is still a headlight floating around somewhere in the River Wye.

In keeping with the theme of the book, one of the curious aspects of this incident was that we should never have been where we were at the time. It was only that I had misread the road map and we were heading for the wrong Newtown, where I was due to play that evening. The reference in the index was page 23 1D, I think, and I spotted Newtown on 1D as I flicked through without checking the page I was on. Believe it or not, in this particular road atlas there are two Newtowns in sections 1D, and I was looking at the one on another page.

While we're on the subject of wrong destinations, poor Doug Mountjoy rang his manager one evening to check final directions: 'I'm in Dartford. Where exactly is this place?' 'Dartford?' came the reply. 'Why not try Dartmouth!'

Alex Higgins was playing me in an exhibition match. I was at the table and Alex was watching every shot I made very intently. During my break, the 'drinks man' came round and asked Alex if he'd like another lager. Needless to say the answer was in the affirmative and the man returned shortly with a pint glass.

Alex held out his hand and took the glass, still with his eyes fixed on what I was doing. As he walked round the table, he started pouring the fresh lager into his original glass. Soon he was pouring the stuff all over the floor, much to everyone's amusement.

Poor Alex was concentrating so much on what I was doing that he didn't notice he had been handed a pint of lager which he was trying to pour into a half-pint mug. It was probably the worst shot he made all evening.

As with all sports, there are stories – sad ones, happy ones, bizarre ones, disastrous ones. Everyone involved has his own tales to tell, for which sport has to be grateful. If for no other reason, at least it proves we are all human although about the man who could hold nine balls in one hand I have my doubts!

PS If anyone can spare a supply of cigars, Father Bill says he'd be most grateful, if I carry on playing the way I do!

MOST
UNLIKELY
IMPLEMENTS

How long is a frame? At village hall level there must be almost no limit, but among the game's senior players it is rare to find someone dawdling for the sake of it. So, while defence experts like Cliff Thorburn and Terry Griffiths have engaged in some lengthy matches over the years, their longest frame could not compare with the 73-minute epic that occupied the Humberside pair, Gary Miller and Stuart Alliston, in 1983. Mind you, they were **using a potato as a cue-ball!**

Then there was the case of the ball which, on being struck, came in half and one of the halves swerved neatly into a pocket. Fortunately for referees, this kind of tricky behaviour is rare among snooker balls – even in the mating season.

The shortest-ever cue (with the shortest-ever playing career) must be the one introduced by Alec Brown in November 1938 at Thurston's Hall, London. It was during the third frame of his heat against Tom Newman in the Daily Mail Gold Cup that Brown landed himself in a bothersome situation.

After potting a red, he left the cue-ball surrounded almost entirely by reds except for a narrow channel to the black which was above its spot. The black was the only colour on, so he was faced with a very awkward stroke which he could make either from the baulk end or by leaning over from one side and using a mid-air bridge.

Brown studied his position carefully, then drew out what looked like a fountain pen from his waistcoat pocket. The spectators wondered what he had in mind, and most probably thought that for some reason not immediately clear to them he was going to measure the distance from the cue-ball to the black, or perhaps he wanted to gauge the precise width of the channel.

To their astonishment, Brown **chalked one end of his 'fountain pen'**

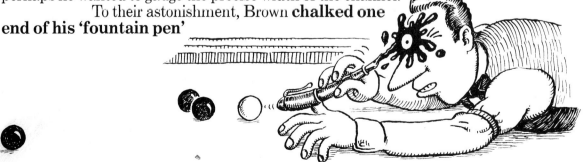

and, leaning over from behind the top cushion, stroked the cue-ball on to the black. As he straightened up, a burst of excited chatter broke from the audience, Newman immediately protested, and Thurston's resident referee, Charlie Chambers, stepped forward to give a ruling.

He asked to see the 'fountain pen' and Brown handed over what he claimed was a proper cue. It was in fact a tiny strip of ebony five inches long which the player's father had made for him, adding an orthodox, if tiny, tip at one end. After Charlie Chambers had examined it, he passed it on to Newman, who promptly put it in his pocket muttering 'This should be useful'. As far as the referee was concerned, however, extremely short cues were against the spirit of the game even if they were not officially outlawed. He walked to the scoreboard and awarded seven points to Newman. Foul stroke.

Eight days later the Billiards Association & Control Council met and a new clause was added to the rules stating that a cue should be no less than three feet in length and should show no substantial departure from its traditional shape and form.

Much more recently, Jimmy White made a move in the opposite direction. It was obviously successful, for when a keen reporter asked him why his game had improved White replied:

'I've put two inches on my cue.'

'What does that mean to you?' asked the reporter.

Helpfully, White explained: 'It's longer.'

Mark Wildman is **no stranger to the elongated implement.**

An antique cue weighs in at an impressive 41 oz.

One evening at the Conservative Club in Peterborough, he was challenged by a local character, a certain Major.

'I'll give you a start of 80,' said the Major, 'on just one condition. What do you think of that?'

'Depends on the condition,' said Mark with justifiable wariness.

'It's very simple,' said the Major. 'I will give you 80, provided I select the cue you play with.'

'Ah,' said Mark, 'but you'll give me one with no tip on it.'

'No, no,' said the Major. 'It will have a tip on it.'

'Well,' thought Mark. 'I can't go too far wrong here.'

He accepted the challenge. The Major went over to the table and pulled out the half-butt. 'Here's your cue,' he said, allowing himself a small smile of triumph.

As well he might. **Playing under the cushion with an eight-foot cue** is no easy feat, and Mark soon found himself out in the street for some shots which could only be got at by aiming through the club's front windows!

Kirk Stevens pulled off another bizarre feat of cuemanship in Malta. He arrived on the island to play in the 1978 World Amateur Championships, but

A rare Stuart billiard table on display at Sotheby's. Former billiards champion Tom Newman watches while opera star Désirée Ellinger tries a shot with the old-style cue.

The well-equipped billiard room of 1781.

then found he was minus his luggage, cue and all. Ever resourceful, he went into action with a two-piece cue made up from a shaft borrowed from one player and a butt belonging to another. This, to Kirk's surprise and pleasure, just about worked, though not when one of the owners was scheduled to play at the same time as he was and wanted his bit back. Anyhow, he struggled on, and to his amazement reached the semi-finals.

Amateurs everywhere, relax. Maybe your cue is not as important as you thought it was. Certainly, anything you decide to play with will not be as eccentric as the implement favoured by Napoleon Bonaparte. In the field of eccentric actions, **the Emperor takes some beating.** The firm of Thurston one day received an unusual gift from the Governor of St Helena – a brass name-plate taken from a billiard table used at Longwood, the house where Napoleon lived during his exile on the island, up to his death in 1821. In Forsythe's *History of Captivity* there is an exterior view of the billiard room, and the author describes how Napoleon spent many evenings playing chess, whist and billiards, and how, at the latter, he preferred using his hand to playing with the cue.

The **stickiest handicap** suffered by any snooker player came about when Willie Thorne split the tip of his cue and used Superglue to put on a new one.

'A blob of the stuff spilled on to the shaft and it was virtually impossible to get off,' he explained, looking a touch cross-eyed after completing a round in the 1984 Jameson International Open tournament at Newcastle. 'Apart from buying a new cue, there was nothing I could do but get used to the idea of playing with a lump in front of my eyes.'

The impact – literally – of New York inventor J. W. Hyatt's celluloid billiard balls, which he patented in 1870, had a bizarre side-effect. Hyatt came up with his new material, the world's first commercial synthetic plastic, after a New York firm offered a prize of $10,000 to anyone who could devise a substitute for ivory balls, which were very expensive and needed regular regrinding to keep them spherical.

Two small drawbacks to the celluloid balls, which were made partly from nitro-cellulose, were that they could be easily set on fire and, when they made sharp contact or were struck too hard, they made a small explosive noise like a percussion guncap. Among the various people who complained about the new balls was a saloon owner. He said he didn't mind the noise itself, but whenever it happened **all his customers pulled a gun.**

Top candidate for the world's highest snooker table is the frozen relic discovered by two climbers in the foothills of Mount Everest. The full-size British-built table was probably installed in the vicinity for use by Army officers, possibly even colleagues of the men stationed at Ootacamund who devised the rules of snooker.

Some bugger's pinched the white!

When a snooker referee has left his marker at home, his best friend is … someone else's teeth. This was the remarkable solution when a player at an Oxfordshire club match asked the referee Dave Oliver to clean the cue-ball. After Oliver had vainly searched his pockets, out of the crowd jumped a man he recognized – Mick Fogarty from Didcot.

Fogarty consulted quickly with the referee, then removed his bottom set and placed them delicately round the ball.

Like Cinderella and the slipper, **teeth and ball were clearly made for each other.** They fitted perfectly.

This was not the first appearance on the green baize of a bottom set. Indeed, sales of ball markers may be threatened if the practice grows, especially in televised matches. Some time ago, during a Ray Reardon exhibition in a Leeds club, referee Ray Crook also resorted to the bottom set of his false teeth to mark the position of a ball while he cleaned it.

This practice does *not* have the support of John Street, Len Ganley or John Williams – or the BBC.

Tom Newman lines up a shot in his match against Test cricketer Jack Hobbs, who had presumably been given the choice of implements.

Should spectacles be allowed to qualify as playing 'implements'? Nowadays, when it is common to find players sporting a pair of the giant panda specs made famous by Dennis Taylor, it is easy to forget that, not so very long ago, there were no special optical aids available, and a player with eyesight problems either played 'blind' or not at all.

The first big change came about before the Second World War, when Fred Davis lost a world championship match because he could not see properly. At the time he thought he would probably have to give up playing. Needless to say, he was very upset about it. So, by the way, was his brother Joe, though for different reasons. Joe saw the defeat as a terrible slight on the good name of the family, and in the next round he took on the same player and beat him by 30 frames to 1, by any standards a crushing margin.

This had the effect of encouraging Fred to try and find a way to continue in the game. Eventually, he half-stumbled across an optician who designed for him the first pair of tip-up snooker specs, with swivel lenses that could be set at whatever angle was right for the player.

John Spencer in experimental mood before an exhibition match with Dennis Taylor.

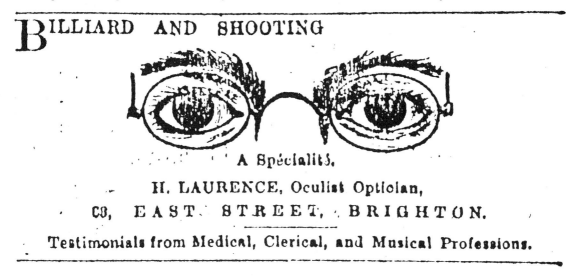

Swivel specs remained the answer until the 'upside-down' design was perfected. These, sitting high on the face, allow the player to look through the optical centre with a minimum of movement. Dennis Taylor has worn his with great success and so has his namesake, David Taylor. All spectacles though, regardless of the advanced technology that goes into their manufacture, are vulnerable. David Taylor found this out in the 1984 Professional Championship at Ipswich. He was due to go out for a match wearing his upside-downs. He put them down on the floor for a moment ... and **his wife trod on them!**

Bill Werbeniuk's unlikely implement is his lager glass, but we will come to that in a moment. First, to explain to anyone not in the know, the well-built Canadian has a nervous tremor in his right hand which he attempts to quieten by **deluging his system with lager.** All other cures have met with no success at all, though he is currently hoping that an Oriental acupuncturist may be able to de-twitch him.

As a result, Werbeniuk must make a huge capital outlay on lager each year if he is to remain among the high prizewinners. In 1981 he succeeded in persuading the Inland Revenue that all this in-tournament guzzling was a legitimate business expense, and he was able to offset £2,000 worth of lager against his earnings. (This allowance was later withdrawn.)

Now to the story. One night at The Crucible, Bill Werbeniuk was extremely agitated. His lager had been delivered to him in a straight glass! Uproar. They sent for Ken Smith, the Mr Fixit of the World Championships, and he speedily arranged for a uniformed police constable to slip down the road to the Brown Bull and requisition four pint mugs with handles. Later, Smith explained what all the fuss was about:

'Bill was perspiring, and with having to hold on to a cold glass he was continually having to wipe his hands and that was spoiling his bridge It might not sound much but, like in the old legend of the golfer being put off his swing by the beating of butterflies' wings in the next meadow, **everything matters at the top.'**

SMART
LADS WANTED,
NO
SCRUFFS

Snooker has always been a dressy game; and so, before it, was billiards. Since Victorian times, players have cultivated a special atmosphere: a clubland image of style and elegance; of low lights and smoking rooms; starched cuffs and shirt fronts, and low-cut waistcoats which until recently could be any colour as long as they were black.

Black was best for two reasons. Billiards and snooker were evening games, something you did after dinner. And the general uniform for evening wear was, rigidly, a black dress suit. Even in the daytime, it was thought a little wild for a gentleman to wear anything other than a frock coat or a morning coat in town. Lounge suits were gradually permitted, and by the 1890s fancy waistcoats were creeping in. But, and this was the second reason for staying sartorially sober, these didn't always suit the wearer. The *Tailor and Cutter* warned its readers:

'Gentlemen with abdominal convexity will use discretion in the

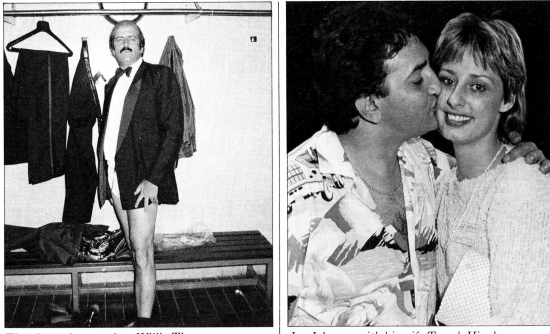

The almost immaculate Willie Thorne.

Joe Johnson with his wife Terryl. His shoes were a highlight of the 1986 World Championship final.

employment of hues and patterns calculated to draw attention to that unromantic formation.'

Unromantic formation. Does that remind you of anybody? Nowadays, of course, the rules are different. We have colour television, and the old regulations about black-and-white no longer apply. Professionals are still required to wear a dress suit for evening matches, and a lounge suit in the afternoon (and that means a three-piecer, with waistcoat). As for colours, though, these may be as dazzling as the player fancies – enough, indeed to rival the ensembles of Louis XIV and his courtiers, who were the **original Flash Harrys of the billiard room.**

One of the finest, and at the same time most disastrous, snooker suits to be seen in recent years was an emerald green velvet outfit designed for Dennis Taylor to wear at the 1974 Norwich Union Open, held at the Piccadilly Hotel, London. Very fine it looked, at first sighting, and there were emerald green shoes to match. Dennis, who was then a fairly new professional, was feeling well pleased with himself – until he went out to play and found there was not a pocket in the entire suit. Nowhere to put his chalk! Disaster!

Not surprisingly, Alex Higgins created some mild tremors in the snooker establishment over the tie he would not wear, or ripped off during play, claiming that his dickie-bow gave him a neck rash – and yes, he would produce a doctor's certificate to back up his claim.

What of the future? At the 1986 World Championships Higgins could still be observed in a tieless state, but his colleagues seemed happy enough conforming to the traditional standard. It is a tricky issue, trickier than it might at first appear. It the authorities do cave in, and permit a general tielessness, much of snooker's **priceless image of slightly antique smartness** would be lost.

Trousers are a different matter. There is little or no dispute over the desirability of players wearing, and not losing, their trousers while play is in progress. John Virgo's problem was that his trousers kept trying to part company with their owner.

He was playing Steve Davis in the fourth round of the 1985 Goya Matchroom Trophy. Lacking a third hand to keep his trousers from slipping beyond the barriers of decency, he lost the first three frames and was not a happy man. To his rescue came referee Len Ganley. He lent Virgo his braces, and Virgo responded by winning the fourth frame. It looked as though his luck was turning, but then the lights went out, and after a ten-minute delay Davis came back to win the match 5 – 1.

Even worse luck befell Canada's Bill Werbeniuk, whose trousers ripped in front of the television cameras during his match against David Taylor in the 1980 World Team Championship. For the viewers this would not have been a pretty spectacle at the best of times – and on this occasion the bulky Werbeniuk was not wearing underpants! Later while he was being stitched together again, his colleague Cliff Thorburn remarked:

'I know it's a needle match, but this is ridiculous.'

With hindsight (?), Werbeniuk could at least console himself that he had achieved a truly bizarre record – the **first professional snooker player to split his pants** while playing on television.

MONEY
MONEY
MONEY
MONEY

It is hardly snooker's fault that the press and television people insist on hanging price tags on everything. Sometimes it seems as though value in £ (or £ million or $ billion) is the only way to measure either people or events. You've seen the lines. Headings like this: 'Millionaire snooker star loses £800 suit, priceless gold cue and $400 champion tortoise in 5 million yen motorway hijack.'

Well, something like that. At least, when the subject under scrutiny is money and sport, there is a legitimate reason for counting all those shekels. What is more, the rise and rise of snooker has undoubtedly been the sporting success of the last decade.

Few people, for instance, have not heard that Steve Davis earns £1 million a year, or some figure so mind-boggling that the odd £50,000 either way seems irrelevant – despite the fact that we wouldn't mind earning that odd £50,000 ourselves. What is perhaps more interesting is to put Steve's earnings into the context of what he used to get a few years ago. Apart from playing snooker, he has only ever had two jobs, one in a butcher's shop and one in a greengrocer's – and the fruit and veg.

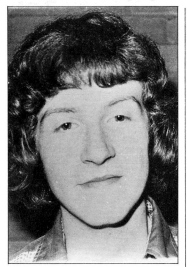

Steve Davis in the days before the big money.

World champion with all the trappings.

business used to pay him 28p an hour. Not a bad increase.

Similarly Dennis Taylor would not have wanted to swap his cheque for winning the 1985 World Championship with what Joe Davis received when he won the first title in 1927. Sixty thousand pounds against six pounds ten (£6.50); an increase of 929,976.92 per cent. Impressive, even if you allow for inflation and the higher earnings which today's professional sportsmen expect to claim. But do they? Among professional snooker players the answer is: not if they are realistic.

To earn big money from snooker you have to be among the top ten players. In the 1983-84 season the average prize-winnings for all professionals was a little under £9,000. If however, you disregard the top ten, the average falls to just over £3,500 – well short of the average national wage. Of course, professional snooker players have other ways of earning money – through exhibition matches, personal appearances, endorsements, and so on – so the average wage-earner need not worry unduly about their plight. In fact, the average wage-earner's best move might be to get in there and compete with the pros.

Snooker is one of those more straightforward sports in which amateurs are able to win prize money, some of it by no means to be sniffed at. When Doug Mountjoy beat John Spencer to win the 1974 Pontins Open, he became the

Joe Davis, world champion for twenty years.

first amateur to win a £1,000 first prize. Another Welsh amateur, Steve Newbury, finished his last season as an amateur (in 1983–4) with winnings in excess of £8,000. Only 22 professionals won more than him that season.

One amateur full of 'start up and go' was Steve Carr from Tyne and Wear, who got himself a government grant to play snooker. Steve had been unemployed since he left school. His future in the job market was highly unpromising, so in 1984 he decided to apply to the Department of Employment for the £40 a week enterprise allowance. This would buy him the time to play snooker full-time, and if all went well Steve had dreams of becoming a professional.

'All right,' said the DoE, somewhat to Steve's surprise, 'you can have

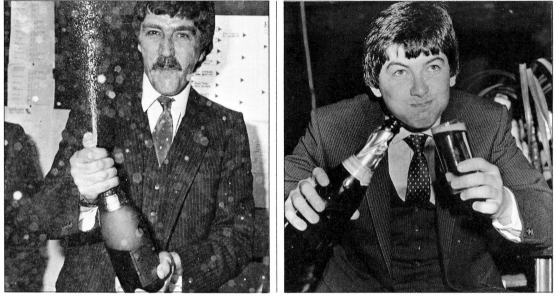

Cliff Thorburn (left), well-practised in the handling of champagne while for John Parrott (right) it seems a more novel experience.

the grant – on two conditions. You must not hustle, and you must not play exhibition matches for as long as you are receiving the allowance.'

'Right,' said a delighted Steve. 'I can live with that!'

Back with the pros, in 1980 it became clear that there was, after all, **a bottom to snooker's treasure pot.** A round-robin tournament was staged at the New London Theatre under the title of 'Champion of Champions'. All the leading players took part, and after competing for about a fortnight Doug Mountjoy emerged as the winner. He duly received the victor's envelope – but there was nothing in it. The tournament had been such a commercial disaster that no money was left to pay the players.

That tournament was one half of a double irony for John Virgo, who had finished as runner-up. In 1983-84 a professional snooker league was started, containing 12 leading professional players, and off they went to tour the country. It seemed such a good idea at the time, but it proved to be prohibitively expensive. The cost of hotels, transport, etc, for the whole circus went way over the budget, and then began to eat into the prize-money. In the end there was no cash left for the winner – John Virgo.

What made it even worse for John was that in those two competitions he had turned in his two best performances in recent years.

If there is anything worse than not being paid, it is **having money taken away from you.** This happens periodically to Alex Higgins, who in May 1982 was fined £1000 for a variety of offences. One of his transgressions was that he had peed into a flower display which was the property of BBC Television.

'Such a shame,' commented producer Mike Adley. 'They were plastic flowers!'

Are you sure these flowers are plastic, Mike?

DO NOT WATER by order B.B.C

FIT FOR
SNOOKER:
SNOOKER
FOR
FITNESS

Even in 1938 the competition among billiards and snooker players was so intense that many felt they should be as fit as footballers or ice hockey players. The leading pros had their own individual methods of keeping themselves in good condition: Joe Davis had a golf handicap of 8, Tom Newman played bowls and a little golf, and Sidney Smith sprinted. Frank Ives, the American, was almost as good on a cycle as he was with a cue. At Hampden Park, Springfield, Mass., he set records for distance events up to 50 miles which remained unbeaten for many years.

World billiards champion Welker Cochran was an enthusiastic baseball player.

Horace Lindrum was different, in fact he had a unique recreation (although he claimed that it didn't keep him fit). He was an **expert marbles player.** He played for so many years that his right thumb became bigger than his left. He could pot, screw back, and cannon with marbles with the same ease as he achieved with billiard balls. For fitness he played tennis!

All-round sportsmen are less easy to find among snooker players, although Eddie Charlton is a notable exception. As a youngster in Australia he was a sports nut, and took part in whatever sport he could, whenever he could. He played senior grade soccer for more than ten years and in 1950 was a member of the Swansea Belmont crew that won the Australian Surfing Championship. Athletics, cricket, boxing and roller-skating were other sports at which Eddie excelled, and in 1956 he and his brother Jim (who is also a professional snooker player in Australia) carried the Olympic torch on its route towards Melbourne.

Dennis Taylor played soccer and Gaelic football, Steve Davis still uses the gym, and Alex Higgins once harboured ambitions as an all-rounder, as we shall shortly see. When he was a youngster, he had wanted to be a jockey rather than a snooker player, and he obtained a place in Newmarket at the stables of trainer Eddie Reavey.

The Hurricane was never a great success on board the horses and was not given a mount at a race meeting. Eventually he was released with a reputation for being 'lazy' and for putting on too much weight.

Alex's great 'alternative' sporting chance came when he was invited to Oliver Reed's house for a **weekend quadrathlon.** The four events were snooker, arm-wrestling, table tennis and non-stop disco dancing. The results of the contest were never recorded in the sporting archives, nor have any other details come to our ears, though we may surmise that the dustman on his next visit found a lot of glass items awaiting removal. On the subject of which, here is a strange case of how positive mental sponsorship can be good for snooker players.

Before 1985, an Irish team had never reached the final of the World Team competition. In that year, however, the All-Ireland trio of Dennis Taylor, Alex Higgins and Eugene Hughes not only reached the final, they beat England 'A' to win the trophy 9–7. Appropriately, the event was being sponsored for the first time by ... Guinness.

One of the best sportsmen outside his own speciality is Cliff Thorburn. Cliff was such a promising golfer that he had the opportunity to turn professional. He finally opted for snooker on the grounds that there were not so

Alex Higgins misses a long pot.

many snooker pros around, and so he must stand a better chance of reaching the top with a cue in his hand rather than a club. He is still a keen amateur golfer and plays off a handicap of 4.

Cliff had a golf match one day against one of the directors of

Where's that one gone? Nick Faldo and Steve Davis look concerned.

Jameson Whiskey. When they had settled the debate over their handicaps, the whiskey man stipulated that they had to play 'Irish rules'.

'Oh,' said Cliff, 'and what are they?'

'We play to the handicaps we have agreed, plus I get two free throws.'

Cliff assumed he was referring to drop-balls, and nodded assent.

At the fourth hole, Cliff played a beautiful second shot to lay his ball up to within a foot of the pin. Whereupon the chap from Jameson walked over, picked up Cliff's ball and **hurled it into some nearby bushes.**

'What's that for?' gasped Cliff.

'That's my first free throw,' explained his opponent.

All professional snooker players find they need some kind of job to keep them going and pay the bills before they are able to rely on snooker as their main source of income. Dennis Taylor recalls going for a job on a building site.

'The foreman said he was looking for a handyman, and could I make tea.

Tea up

"Yes," I said, "the best tea in Ireland."

"Can you drive a forklift truck?" asked the foreman.

"Why," says I, "how heavy is the teapot?"'

Few players, however, can have done anything quite as physical as Graham Cripsey of Skegness. Graham, his mother, father and brother Gary were all members of a Wall of Death team that toured the local fairgrounds. Graham remained happily stuck on the centrifugal force game for thirteen years. 'Much easier than earning a living from snooker,' he is quoted as saying.

Tony Knowles, a keen follower of American Football.

At the beginning of 1978, Peter Sayer's main job was scoring goals for Cardiff City FC. For relaxation he played snooker at Llandaff Institute and was a prominent member of the 'C' team, who that season were playing well and were in line for promotion in the local snooker league. When the news broke in February that Peter was being transferred to Brighton for £100,000, his mates at the Institute were horrified, and filed a not-altogether-serious demand for a cut of the transfer fee. The club listened sympathetically but declined to pay out, claiming that since Brighton thought they were buying a 100 per cent footballer, they would prefer to keep 100 per cent of the money.

Should anyone need it, we can offer medical proof that billiards and snooker are good for the health. George Gray, the heavy-scoring Australian billiards player, might never have taken up the game that made him famous if he had not suffered a serious fall while playing in the park one day when he was about twelve years old. Examination revealed a compound fracture of the left arm, and George was duly strapped up in accordance with the medical customs of the day (this was just after the turn of the century). The arm responded to treatment but remained painfully stiff, so George's doctor recommended that he should try playing billiards. That was how he began. At the age of 19 he came to Britain for the 1910–11 season and ran up an astonishing series of breaks, including 23 of more than 1000. Well played, the doctor!

In World War I, billiards was highly thought of in the military hospitals. It was good for morale and it gave recuperating soldiers the kind of light exercise they needed. It also rescued the fortunes of George Nelson, a sales representative with one of the largest manufacturers of billiard tables who was laid off when the demand for tables declined with the advent of war.

George decided that there must still be a market for the game of billiards; having nine children to feed, and no other source of income, he resolved to go into business on his own. He soon discovered that the military hospitals, heavily populated with bored young men waiting for their bodies to mend, were a natural home for his billiard tables. He supplied no fewer than six tables to Beckett Park Hospital in Leeds, four of them for the use of the German internees.

The British soldiers would have bought more tables, but money was tight and at first they could not even raise enough funds to pay for the two they did eventually purchase. George, however, suspecting that the Germans were worth more than they cared to admit, craftily adjusted his prices so that they in effect subsidized the tables which he suppplied to the 'home' players.

Finally, **how fit is a snooker referee?** Obviously, there is no single answer to this, but we do at least know that they have to do a lot of standing about and a surprising amount of walking. In 1984 John Street, a World Championship referee, wore a pedometer to measure his progress through a 25-frame match. At

the end of it, the meter showed that he had covered approximately four miles. Not a huge distance, admittedly, but when you consider that it is nearly as far as a soccer referee travels in the course of an average 90-minute game, it must be enough to keep a man in decent physical shape.

The great thing is not to weaken. At the age of 90, W. J. Peall was having a game of billiards when he missed potting a red off the spot.

'Oh,' he said, 'I'd have got that with my eyes shut fifty years ago.'

A fine figure of a referee – Len Ganley about to put in a spell of training between matches.

BIZARRE
COMPETITORS
&
PLAYING
HABITS

Most bizarre playing habits.

HAIRIEST OPPONENTS

Fred Davis turned up at the Spectrum Arena, Warrington, for his qualifying match in the 1984–85 Mercantile Credit Classic, to find that a chimpanzee from a local circus had wandered into the snooker area and was sitting there waiting for play to start. When he saw the friendly-looking animal, Fred asked: 'Is that my opponent?'

On being assured that it was not, he added: 'Well, there are so many new professionals these days, I don't know half of them.'

Had the chimpanzee been able to play snooker, it would not have been the first time that one of our oldest relations had mastered the sport. In July 1914 *Billiards* magazine reported:

'Among the holiday attractions at the Anglo-American Exposition in Shepherd's Bush is stated to be a monkey that, among other attainments, can play billiards.'

He should have one foot on the ground.

THINNEST COMPETITION

The world Professional Championships have consisted, on three occasions, of just two competitors.

The first time was in 1931 when Joe Davis beat Tom Dennis in the back room of Dennis's Nottingham pub, and the second was three years later when Davis beat Tom Newman in the final.

In 1952 just two men, Horace Lindrum and Clark McConachy, contested the final after all the other leading professionals had boycotted the Championship.

DOZIEST MATCH

During the 1985 Dulux British Open Tony Knowles raised a few eyebrows when, during his match with

Tony Meo, he left the arena. Fed up with Meo's slow play, he decided to go back to the dressing-room for a rest.

'After all,' he said, 'if Meo can take a rest during a game, then why can't I?'

WHITEST CHAMPIONSHIP CONTENDER

National Coach Jack Karnehm is the only person to have been 'whitewashed' three times in the World Professional Championship. John Pulman (1974), Dennis Taylor (1977) and Roy Andrewartha (1978) inflicted these embarrassing defeats upon Karnehm. But none of them detracts from his great skills as a coach.

BLUEST NOTES

These were sounded by Steve Davis after he was surprisingly humiliated 10–1 in the first round of the 1982 World Championships at The Crucible by the then unknown Tony Knowles. Steve wound down by going to a piano teacher and playing the piano for hours every day for the rest of the fortnight.

MOST REVILED OPPONENT

The reputations of some of today's snooker players attract a great deal of attention from the media. But most of them appear as angels compared with Melbourne Inman, billiards champion at the turn of the century.

After beating Tom Reece to win the English Billiards Championship in 1910, he was presented with his trophy by Lord Alverston, the man who sentenced Crippen to death. Later, Reece said: 'If Lord Alverston knew as much about Inman's activities as I do, he'd have given the cup to Crippen, and sent Inman to the gallows.'

BIGGEST HANDS

How many full-sized billiard or snooker balls can you pick up with one hand without the assistance of the cushion? An average man can expect to pick up five balls having a diameter of two and three thirty-seconds inches. George Hunt, a professional from Barnsley, proved himself an exceptional man when he picked up nine.

Highest average age – in the Grandfathers' Club at the Elephant and Castle, 1949.

STRANGEST TABLE MANNERS

Bernard Franks was once asked to officiate at one of the many exhibitions given by that great Irish entertainer, Jackie Rea.

In those days Rea used to take his own set of balls with him, which, though a common occurrence nowadays, was then something of a rarity. Bernard knew that Jackie always liked to use his own set, and as he was taking them out of the box and placing them on the table, he turned to Rea and said:

'Thanks, you've just won me a fiver.'

'How's that?' asked Rea.

Bernard replied: 'I bet some guy in the audience that I'd have your balls in my hands before the night was out.'

MOST LONG-WINDED PLAYER

They don't call Cliff Thorburn 'The Grinder' for nothing. Ask Terry Griffiths, Kirk Stevens and Tony Knowles. In his matches against those three in the 1983 World Professional Championships, he required a total of 17 hours 21 minutes – and plenty of sleep in between – to finish them off.

The meeting with Griffiths lasted a staggering 6 hours 25 minutes and finished at 3.51 am. The quarter-final win over Stevens was 14 minutes shorter, and finished at 2.12 am. Compared with those two, the semi-final against Knowles was a sprint, taking only 4 hours 45 minutes.

By the time he reached the final, Thorburn was feeling understandably fatigued. Steve Davis beat him 18-6.

MOST HI-TECH PLAYER

Since 1985 scientists at Bristol University have been looking to snooker for ways of resolving some of the problems that have held back robots in industry.

They believe that if they can develop a snooker-playing robot, capable of seeing and hitting a ball, they will then be able to reapply these skills to a range of industrial functions.

Professor Richard Gregory, who runs the University's Brain and Perception Laboratory, got the idea from Charles Huff, a BBC snooker producer.

'It sounds like fun,' he said when the project was launched, 'but it will be pushing technology to the limit. The eye will be a television camera. We will start with a standard robotic arm and adapt it to a vision system. It will have to be capable of sensing colour and position.'

We wish them well, but cannot help wondering what will happen if the robots get so efficient that they can knock off century breaks, even strings of 147s, at the press of a button.

AMATEURS' CORNER:
DISASTERS
ALL THE WAY

We are in the Old Gaol Leisure Centre in Abingdon, gathered to explore the nature of disaster as experienced by the average billiards and snooker player. Well, below average in our case, but that could have its advantages.

We have hired a table for two hours and plan to play roughly equal periods of snooker and billiards, followed by a quick burst of bar billiards at our local pub and a few rounds of pool at John's house to close the evening. If, by then, we have not **summoned the Demon Disaster** in a selection of his most vivid cushion-biting, cue-thumping, Aaarrgh-screaming, I-don't-bloody-belieeeeve-it! guises, we will have surprised ourselves.

Already, as we pay at the desk, collect our cues and walk up to the Snooker Room, there has been the odd inkling that we are in appropriate mental shape for our peculiar tournament. For one thing, we – that is, John, Pete, Barry and Webster – nearly failed to meet up in the first place. Contact was finally made when Barry and Webster, cruising down a narrow country lane in Barry's car, met John and Pete coming the other way in John's car. Much stamping on the brakes, then both parties reversed rapidly out of each other's sight. When we at last achieved a perfect rendezvous, Barry said to Pete:

'You said last night we'd meet outside the pub.'

Webster interrupted: 'He said to me we'd meet at John's house. Then he said we'd go there in his car. So why is he sitting in John's car now and not his own?'

Pete said: 'That's cos my car broke down, dinnit, just as I was leaving.'

John said: 'We pushed his car back into his drive, then went round to Webster's in mine. (Turning to Webster.) But you'd left.'

Webster said: 'Of course I'd left. I wasn't meant to be there. I was on my way to your place when I saw Barry outside the pub.'

And so on for a couple more minutes while we all got into John's car and drove to Abingdon. Confusion rather than Disaster; still, it was promising.

We had agreed in advance to play foursomes. Who would go with who? Webster said: 'If we were seeded one to four, I would be four.' There being no argument about that, it was agreed that Webster (best-ever break 7) would play with Pete ('About 40'), leaving John ('18, I think') to partner Barry ('Haven't a clue').

Pete won the toss and elected to break. He did so. John played, followed by Webster, followed by Barry. All the reds remained on the table. A second round of play was completed; all was still intact except that Webster's cue-ball had taken a nasty deflection into the top-left bag. 4 – 0. The first disaster? Perhaps, but not really. The players were not warmed up yet, and you cannot have a real disaster unless there is a bit of passion in the air. Also, Webster is such a dismal player at the best of times, it may have been a mistake to ask him along. The thought arises: below a certain level of play, there is no such thing as 'a disaster', a singular moment when one spectacular piece of bad play or ill-fortune turns a match; below a certain level of play, every shot is a potential, if minor, disaster, one more in a **remorseless chain of incompetence** that continues until the frame is sealed in the opponent's favour.

Possibly. But are these not unduly harsh words? Everyone has to start somewhere, and just because a relative novice has a high striking rate in minor disasters does not mean he is incapable of producing the occasional, and infinitely more memorable, triumph. As we shall see, the Triumph Factor is a powerful influence.

The rest of the frame was basically undramatic, though everyone seemed to have his moments, the petty disasters punctuated by brief triumphs which, nonetheless, in the eye of the shot-maker were of rare beauty – the diamond on a conveyor belt of gravel. Some key statistics may hint at the pace of the play and the tension generated. After eight minutes, the first red was potted; after twenty-two minutes, the first colour went down; after forty-eight minutes, only the black remained. John to play.

'Go for it, John,' cried Barry.

The black was five or six inches to the left of its spot and behind it, about halfway back to the cushion. The white was in the D on the left-hand side. John took up position, bringing the match on the other table to a halt as he did so. (Space is a little tight at the Old Gaol, especially between the two tables which are placed end to end with only a couple of feet between them. We noticed, also, that at the other end of our table you could find yourself playing a 'Fire Alarm' shot in which the butt of the cue breaks the glass and then, presumably, while you play on the room fills up with men in waders, bearing hosepipes.)

So now, the other match being halted, six pairs of eyes rather than four were focussed on the play. John bent ever lower in his best sharpshooting pose, squinting along the barrel, face screwed up in concentration. He made four preliminary passes, then he went for it.

The cue-ball cantered down the table, ignored the black by several clear millimetres, came back off the cushion and returned roughly whence it had come. John buried his head in his left arm, feigning the broken man. 'Ugh-huh-huh-huh!' he sobbed, but no crocodile tears could mask the fact that he was privately horrified and, what was more, this was the evening's First True Disaster. **A glaring foul-up** when the player was under no more than mild pressure. Seven points had been sacrificed and with them the chance of victory – provided the opposition in the shape of Webster refrained from adding to his total of foul shots and provided Pete eventually potted the black (after Barry had missed it). All three performed their parts exactly, and after fifty minutes the frame was over.

First victory to Pete and Webster, 47 – 39. Highest break, 9. It had been a non-electrifying start to the evening, with more weak shots than downright horrible ones, but it would be a foolish man who predicted what these players were capable of doing next.

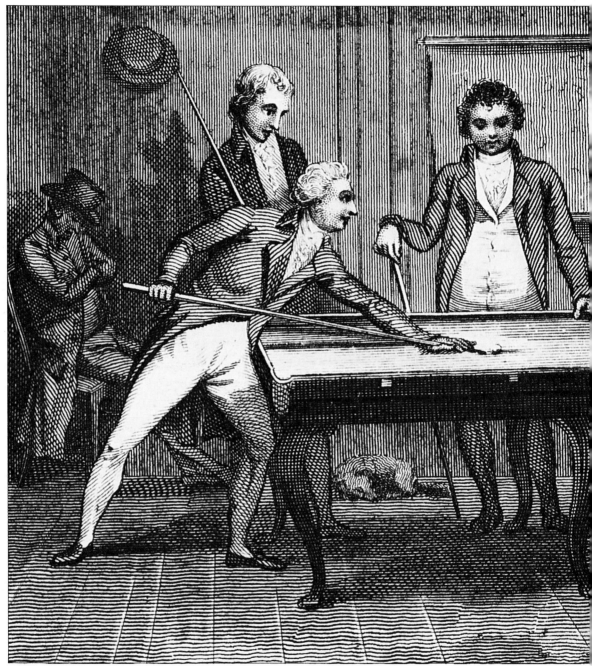

A dignified beginning.

Now they withdrew to the bar which had opened, rather inconveniently, twenty minutes earlier when all the colours were on the table. There followed a brief analysis of the play to date. Pete seemed pleased that his team had won, but felt he should tell Webster that he had contributed 26 points to the opposition's score. Webster countered by saying that he might seem a bit of a

A spot of gamesmanship.

disaster to someone of Pete's exalted ability (potentially divisive sarcasm here, noted the other two), but he could only recall hitting four in-offs and one miss-ball, which was 20 points, a considerably smaller percentage of their total.

John attempted to dilute his own disaster on the black by saying, a trifle darkly, that **this might turn out not to be his night.** (Fifty minutes of play and already he was leaning on Fate to save his reputation.) Barry announced that his pint was particularly welcome because he was suffering from the remnants of a hangover induced the previous night while entertaining some French people. He did not usually drink brandy, he said, and would not have lined his stomach with six pints of bitter before sitting down to dinner with the French people if he could have foreseen the consequences. However, during the closing minutes of the frame he had sensed his vision was becoming sharper and more generally bifocal.

The players refilled their glasses and went back for a second round of action. Now they would test their potential for disaster at billiards.

It was extraordinary how quickly a mood of contentment spread over the company. After the dash and dazzle of snooker, billiards was almost restful. Although the in-offs did not drop as easily as they had done in the snooker game, everyone was rattling up twos and threes and sixes, and Pete had a thirteen. Barry's eyes had come back into line, and although he still preferred using the rest rather than risk standing on one leg to play those awkward shots, his game had measurably improved.

Soon Pete and Webster were leading 55 – 25. Whereupon the flood of

Passions rise.

scoring (a relative term, you understand) dried to mean dribble for Pete and Webster and to nothing at all for the other two. Scoring chances abounded, but for fully ten minutes the players languished in that void where 'The bugger won't go in'.

It was John who set the scoreboard moving again with one of his 'trick shots', as his opponents unkindly called anything that missed the object-ball and/or landed on the floor.

'You *stupid* ball,' he told it, which down Berkshire way is strong stuff, though not strong enough to halt the renewed flow of scoring by the other side. Soon Pete was saying:

'Come on, John, get yourself moving.'

'Why? What's the score?'

'We've got 82 and you've got 33.'

'You're not cheating, are you?'

'We don't have to.'

'I see,' said John. He turned to his partner. 'Right, Barry. I think we'd **better go for a scoobie**.'

Quiet confidence from the experienced player.

This is not so much a well-known billiards term as John's private word for something that does the trick. The new washer that fixes the tap, the cutter that cuts the cigar, the invitation card – all, in their way, are scoobies. At the billiards table, a scoobie was undoubtedly something magical that would unfreeze John and Barry from their present scoring difficulties and set their tally racing.

Barry understood what was required, but had certain doubts. 'I don't mind us doing a scoobie, John, but first we need to find out what it is.'

'No problem, sport,' said John, leaning over the table to play the next shot. He lined himself up for an in-off which called for some right-hand side. Whether, in winding himself up, he neglected to do the same for the cue-ball we cannot say, but when struck it flew past the object-ball on the wrong side and vanished into a far-off pocket with the speed and sureness of a rabbit beating a Jack Russell to its door by a short length.

'Aaarrgh!' yelled Barry.

'Oh, crikey me!' said John. 'What a *?!!-up!'

An emphatic disaster, it had the doubly undermining effect of shaking team morale and extinguishing any faith they might have had in natural magic. Scoobies, for the time being, were out.

Play continued, but for the next couple of rounds it seemed as though the spirits of both teams had been dampened by the failure of the scoobie to show up when invoked, and **scorelessness pervaded the table**. It was Barry whose spirits were the first to revive.

'Come on, John,' he said. 'We only need one good score.'

'What?' said Pete, determined to hang on to his lead, now grown to sixty points. '*One* good score?'

'One *very* good score,' Barry corrected himself.

At this juncture, time suddenly became a big factor in our game. In eight minutes we would have to surrender the table. Attitudes sharpened, which in effect meant that everyone started urging his partner to pull something out quick. No further disasters were committed, and with two minutes remaining Pete announced that he and Webster led by 106 – 36.

'Thirty-eight,' said Barry.

'Are you sure?' said Pete fiercely.

Barry nodded. And, there being no further pots, cannons, flukes or misses, that was the final score.

On now to the third round: a game of bar billiards at the local. For domestic reasons (it was the night of his weekly swimming lesson) Barry now had to leave the group and his place was taken by Edwin, the landlord, who partnered Pete, leaving John and Webster to do the best they could. Edwin entered quickly into the spirit of things.

'Don't knock them sticks down, John!' he shouted, as John prepared to make the opening shot. 'Heh, heh, heh, heh, heh!'

For once that night, John did as he intended. Soon the scores were rattling along. Even Webster, faced with a cluster of balls behind the side or 30 hole, contrived to sink three with one hit.

'Woo-hooh! Nonchalant!' shouted Edwin.

Possibly the whirr of the timing device, set to County League regulations at sixteen minutes, spurred the players to quicken their efforts; certainly the game proceeded at a scampering pace. Pete, especially, had the knack of reaching down for his next ball almost before he had dispatched the last one. After the restful spaciousness of playing billliards on a full-sized table, bar billiards was instant and punchy, and the scoring was stratospheric. One or two white sticks, guarding the 100 holes, fell, cancelling the value of the break, but there was little time for feelings or expressions of sorrow, and the familiar strangled cry of the bandit going over the cliff – 'Aieeeeeee!' – was heard only once during the whole game. Certainly, there was no time for a real sense of disaster to develop and **spread its inhibiting fog** over the player responsible. With bar billiards it was all 'Quick, Edwin, your go. *Cummon*, Edwin, we

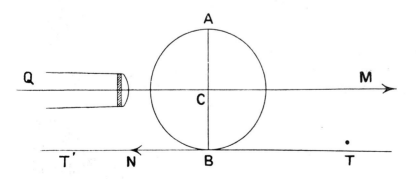

haven't got all night.' 'He's worried about his other customers.' 'He should be, he's only got two.' 'Oh! Bad luck, Edwin. Right, Webster, your go. *Cummon*, Webster, we haven't got all night …'

All too soon the bar dropped, and Edwin was advising: 'Now then, Webster, knock that black stick down and you double your score. Heh, heh, heh, heh, heh!'

'Plonk,' went the final ball. Disaster averted and game over. Pete and Edwin, 1330 points, John and Webster 960. There is something sad about a bar billiards table at the end of a game. Devoid of balls, two sticks blocking the 100s, it looks like a sportsfield after the spectators have gone home. Oh well, no time for philosophy, it's off to John's house to do the pool game.

Edwin was left behind to look after his other customers and we were now joined by Frank, John's brother. It was agreed that they would play together, and Pete and Webster rejoined forces.

This was more serious than the bar billiards. John won the toss and chose to break. 'Right,' he said, 'I'll go.' Adding, 'Got to get something right.'

He went.

'Well,' said Pete, 'you got that wrong.'

Then Pete went, but did no better. 'It's playing on all these different tables,' he explained. 'Short tables, long tables, medium tables … I don't know where I am.'

Nor, it seemed, did John, who was drawing no joy from having home advantage. It being a night for exploring the disasters of the green baize, this was not entirely out of place. It was noticeable, though, that every time he needed that little edge of luck to help his shot, he was denied it. Even when Webster presented him with two shots, he immmediately glided in-off.

Frank noticed, too. 'Why didn't you give it **one of your usual woof-woofs?**' he asked his brother.

John shook his head. 'Should have, really,' he said, but his voice carried no suggestion that it would have made any difference.

The doomed man played on, but there could only be one outcome. 'What more can I say?' he asked helplessly as Pete sank the black. He lapsed into mad giggles.

Another game was played, but the exercise – the seeking-out of disasters – was over. Case proven. The first law of amateur (very amateur) snooker could be written as follows: 'If it's not your night, squire, it's not your night. RIP.'

The problems of precision play.

There was a funny postscript to all this. The next night, Pete and Webster went round to John's house for a few rounds of pool. John's game was altogether different; full of good shots which came off. In the finishing stages of the final game he was snookered from the black by his opponent's sole remaining ball.

Without hesitation, John played the perfect screw shot. The cue-ball fizzed round the opposing ball with all the confidence of Stanley Matthews in his prime, cracked against the black at the perfect spot and sent it wheeling into the pocket.

When the uproar died down, we sensed that we had seen many things. To settle a local matter first, it was definitely a scoobie – no question. So they did exist for snooker players, after all. On a more universal level, we had witnessed the complete reversal, in twenty-four hours, of a player's fortunes – **from black disaster to glowing triumph.** Unbelievable.

John was still chuckling about it a week later. 'No problem, sport,' he said, 'I can live off that for three months.'

There, surely, is the basis for another law of snooker, more important than the first:

'The triumphs are always greater than the disasters.'

GRIEVOUS
BODILY SNOOKER

No great harm should befall a player who carefully minds his Ps and Cues but in every bunch of snooker heroes there is always some daring so-and-so who doesn't mind a quick lunge into the unknown. As a result of which, he may find himself suddenly in need of friends.

Alex Higgins is one who seldom strays far from the gaze of the headline writers. In 1963, after beating Norman Squire, a 63-year-old former Australian champion, in an exhibition match in Sydney, Higgins said of his opponent:

'He's nothing but an old has-been.'

Squire's admirers, taking exception to this tribute, intercepted Higgins and **threw him bodily into the gutter**. There he was made to sit until he had retracted all that he had said. For reasons unknown, the apology was written on toilet paper.

Twenty-three years later, the leopard had not changed his spots. Higgins appeared at the 1986 Mercantile Credit classic sporting a 'shiner' which he blamed on a horse called Dreadnought. Even Dreadnought's owner backed up the story, adding that Higgins was not an experienced horseman and had not been able to handle the horse (forgetting to mention that Higgins had served an apprenticeship at Newmarket under trainer Eddie Reavey).

One in the mouth for Alex Higgins.

This version of events survived for a short while, but then was fatally kicked in the head when fellow snooker professional Paul Medati declared that the story was in essence correct, except that *he* had played the role of Dreadnought.

In other quarters they talk of the night when a vindaloo curry, on the one hand, and a Pyrenean Mountain dog on the other, were the instruments that tempted Higgins into trouble.

One evening in about 1980 Alex settled down in his hotel to a supper consisting of steak and vindaloo curry. He noticed that the steak had a strip of fat on it which he did not intend to eat, and he also could hardly fail to notice that a Pyrenean Mountain dog – one of those massive white cousins of the St Bernard – was pacing around the room. A generous man, Alex cut off a piece of fat, put some curry on it and gave it to the dog.

The dog liked it and came back for more. Alex would gladly have provided a second helping, but was forestalled by the dog's owner, a cross-looking lady who hauled her animal away from Higgins's table and abruptly ordered our hero to desist from feeding the dog. She retired behind a partition to the bar.

Minutes later, Higgins followed the same path to get himself another drink. Out of sight of the snooker gossips, brisk words were exchanged between Alex and the lady's husband, and **a fist or two must have flown** because when Alex returned to his place he was sporting the beginnings of a black eye.

This was a story which the press hounds never quite got hold of; they knew that something had happened, but were unable to pin down precisely what. Today, alas, they are more vigilant.

In the more robust world of pool, players are less concerned about concealing what they get up to. At the first-ever organized pool championship in Wolverhampton, a motley bunch had gathered. During the first match a player got down and fouled a ball with his sleeve.

The referee called: 'Foul stroke.'

The player looked astounded. 'Foul stroke?' he said. 'How the —— hell can it be a foul stroke when I haven't even —— started?'

Soon a free-for-all began, which obviously suited some contestants far more than playing pool. There were bodies on the floor and the pool contest was abandoned.

If you want to be famous for a short time, and earn yourself some

Words of caution for Terry Griffiths from referee John Williams.

space in a national newspaper – even if it's only one and three-sixteenths inches in the *Daily Mail* – try throwing two billiard balls through a window of No. 10 Downing Street. This was what Arnold Barraclough did in November 1970, when he was 35 and would not give his address. At Bow Street Magistrates' Court, London, he was remanded in custody for a medical report.

And now, **Oral Snooker**. There are various ways of making a newsworthy contribution to this branch of the sport, and the following story makes it quite clear that spectators should always stand well back from the table.

A spectator at a pool game at the George Hotel in Bridlington was highly amused when his friend missed the final black. He laughed so much that he doubled up, and while clutching at his stomach must have activated his anti-choke mechanism – whereupon his false teeth jumped out and fell down a pocket.

This is particularly unfortunate with pool, because keys are then needed to open the table. At the hostelry in question they had none, and an engineer had to make a forty-mile journey to liberate the teeth.

More serious is the bar stunt of putting a snooker ball in one's mouth. History has shown that the ball does not easily go in, and sometimes it fails to come out. As long ago as 1894 *Billiards* magazine reported this incident:

'…a man boasted that he could place a billiard ball in his mouth and at the first attempt accomplished the feat. The second time, however, he failed to extricate the ball; and, amid considerable excitement, the man was removed to Middlesex Hospital but died on the way. **This man's mouth was evidently much larger than his intelligence**.'

In December 1984, a pool player in Cornwall tried the same trick in a last-ditch effort to stop his opponents from winning the game. In went the white, and everyone laughed. Everyone laughed, and laughed, until, eyes popping, the keeper of the ball went purple in the face and collapsed on the floor. As the laughter died away, a part-time fireman gave him the kiss of life, an ambulance rushed him to hospital and, some time later, a doctor managed to free the ball.

When he came to, the pool player complained: 'The nurses are taking the micky out of me something rotten.'

We can only imagine some of the things they may have said.

Ray Reardon tells an equally chilling story from his boyhood days in Tredegar. Archie was a bit on the simple side, and when Ray and three friends bet him sixpence that he could not get a billiard ball into his mouth he popped one in without a second thought. Where it stuck.

There being no way the boys could extricate the ball from its lodging place behind Archie's teeth, they led the winner of the bet, now gurgling ominously and turning a faint shade of blue, to the local hospital. Several front teeth had to be removed before the ball was freed. Recalling the incident, Ray was once heard to say:

'Best tanner's worth I ever had!'

Neighbourhood patrols are a helpful way of keeping law and order – provided everyone on the same side knows what everyone else is doing. Timothy, a vigilante in Chelmsley, West Midlands, took his trusty snooker cue with him one night. His target: a local flasher. As he softly padded the streets and back alleys he spotted a dark shape crouched beside a fence. Slowly he crept towards the shape, then dashed the last few feet and **smote it heavily about the head with his cue.**

Two things then happened in rapid succession. The crouching intruder fell sideways on to the pavement, muttering the words: 'I'm a police officer.' Then the fangs of the police officer's dog sank into Timothy's bottom. Minutes later he was lying on the ground, handcuffed, on his way to a night in the cells. At Solihull Magistrates' Court, the beaks ruled that Timothy had been too quick on the draw, despite his plea that 'The police didn't tell us they had left a man in hiding.' He had to pay a fine plus compensation to the police officer who, not surprisingly, had suffered dizzy spells after the attack.

Ultimate billiard violence was the climax of a rough evening between two Frenchmen in 1834. Monsieur Lenfant and Monsieur Mellant began their match quietly enough, but all too soon an 'atmosphere' arose. From ill-tempered bickering the situation worsened. Voices were raised, cues flung down and a passionate argument raged between the two men. Neither was prepared to be reasonable; each was determined to tear a bigger strip off the other, and matters quickly reached a point where the honour of both men had been thoroughly dipped in the sludge. Only one remedy would suffice – a duel.

The two hotheads could not be persuaded to wait and allow a cooling-down period. Pistols at dawn seemed to them like cowardly procrastination. They wanted to settle their quarrel there and then. For the first time that evening they reached an agreement. They would stage their duel in the very room in which they stood: their weapons would be billiard balls at 10 paces.

They drew lots to see who should throw first. The winner was Monsieur Mellant. While his adversary, Monsieur Lenfant, took up position 10

paces away, he picked up the red ball from the table, then drew back his arm, took careful aim and hurled the ivory missile. It caught Lenfant straight between the eyes, killing him instantly.

THE CIRCUS COMES TO TOWN

When we see them in action, we see them at their best – true 'knights of the green baize cloth'. It is only in the intervals between play, when these great champions are attempting to rest or find their way from one venue to another, that we can occasionally detect their human fallibility.

As when Jimmy White got off the train at Warrington for the 1986 Mercantile Credit Classic. Who knows what weighty thoughts were distracting him as he took his place in the queue at the taxi rank. After twenty minutes he had reached the head of the queue and soon a taxi drew up.

'Patten Arms Hotel, please,' said White as he opened the door.

The driver responded with a quick gesture meaning 'Hold on'. Then he pointed across the road to a large sign. It said: 'Patten Arms'. White had been standing in the taxi queue looking at his destination for twenty minutes. It served him right for skipping school and going to Zans Hall Billiard Club instead...

This club was a major landmark in Jimmy White's map of the known world when he was a pupil at the Ernest Bevin Comprehensive School, Tooting. He

Jimmy White struggles with another testing situation.

had early set his heart on becoming a snooker player, and as time went by his practice sessions at Zans began to collide more and more with school lessons. This brought him into increasing conflict with the authorities, often represented by Mr Beattie, Jimmy's headmaster.

Concerned as he was at Jimmy's determination to **leave shool minus an education**, Mr Beattie felt that little or nothing would be achieved by a 'big stick' approach. He opted instead for the 'carrot on a stick' and he and Jimmy

made a deal. If the boy went to school for morning lessons, he would be allowed out at dinner time to play snooker.

This is what happened, and this is why Jimmy emerged from his schooldays with a brilliant future set realistically in his sights. This is also why, from time to time, he hails taxis in funny places.

There was nothing new about Jimmy's aberration. Knights of the green baize have been at odds with the rest of the world over their travelling arrangements since the turn of the century, and possibly before.

On Saturday 14 September 1901, the great William J. Peall, spot-stroke king and self-styled **'Champion of Ordinary Billiards'**, was summoned before Reigate Magistrates on a charge of speeding. Police witnesses claimed they had set a trap near Redhill to catch

motorists and that other dangerously fast breed, cyclists; according to their timing methods, Peall had been driving a great deal faster than the permitted maximum of 12 mph. He was fined £2 plus costs. *The World of Billiards* devoted a full page to the affair, including a cartoon, and another source reports that during his case Peall, who was just five feet tall, was ordered tersely by the Chairman of the Bench to stand up. Peall replied:

'With due respect, sir, I *am* standing up.'

The report could not resist commenting that 'having to use the rest as much as he did, it is remarkable that he achieved such pre-eminence.'

On occasion, the confused travellers can be the snooker reporters themselves. On their way to the 1984 Benson & Hedges Irish Masters tournament, Terry Smith of the *Daily Mirror* and Graham Nickless of the *Daily Star* crossed the tarmac at Heathrow Airport and started climbing the steps to their plane. Halfway up they were startled to realize that a sudden outburst of car horns and people shouting was aimed at them. They stopped, and were told that the steps did not lead up to a plane, in fact they went nowhere. When they eventually boarded the plane, they were greeted by an Aer Lingus hostess who said:

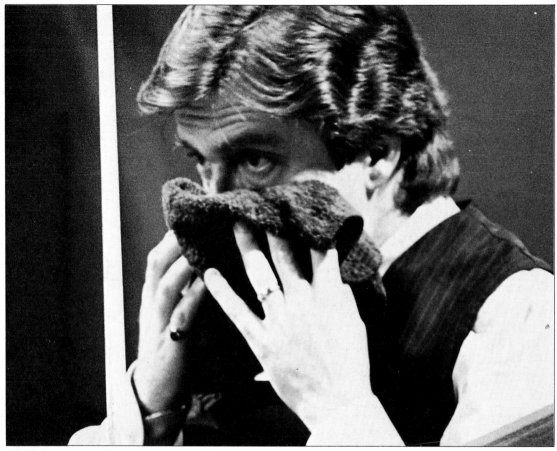

Cliff Thorburn trying to avoid recognition.

'Good morning, gentlemen. You've just taken today's **Aer Lingus intelligence test** – and failed!'

When he was 'on the road', playing snooker from town to town to earn money, Cliff Thorburn soon realized that it paid not to let people know who you were or what your game was. His method of sinking into the background was to disguise himself in a pair of garage overalls. Whenever he arrived in a new town, he would make a note of the name of a garage and use it if anyone asked where he worked.

One evening, he had just finished a match and was pocketing his winnings when his opponent said:

'You're pretty good, kid. Pretty good. Where do you work?'

'I'm at Henderson's,' said Cliff, who had done his usual homework.

'The hell you are,' said the guy. 'I *am* Henderson.'

Cliff now prizes that moment as one of the most embarrassing of his life.

A man lost for words is not quite the same as a man who disappears altogether. As yet, no-one seems to know what happened to Sudan's entrant in the 1985 World Amateur Championships, Victor Yassa. Word has it that visa problems

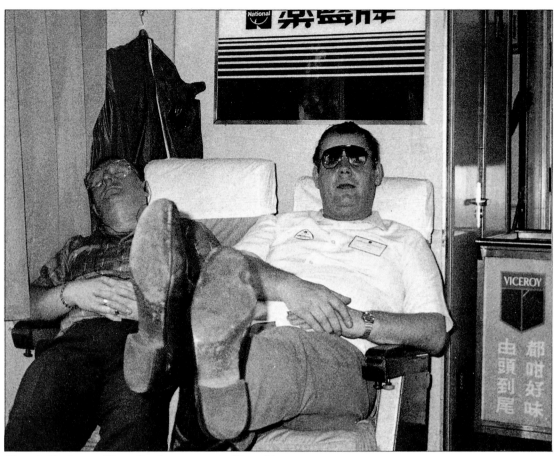

Dennis Taylor and Len Ganley on tour in Hong Kong.

prevented him from getting to Blackpool. If they did, it was news to the Sudanese Embassy in London, who rang up the tournament to find out how 'our boy' was doing.

A more famous no-show was that of Alex Higgins, who failed to turn up for a presentation after a major event. Dennis Taylor explained his absence by saying:

'He's gone to Belfast to launch a ship but he won't let go of the bottle.'

John Spencer once put an unfortunate strain on the bonds of friendship when he arranged for a party of thirty well-wishers from the Bolton area to watch him play at Derby during the 1983 Yamaha Masters. He arranged a coach and even provided the tickets. The only problem was, the tickets were for the previous day's play.

The touring life is full of scheduling disasters. The dates in a player's diary need only be a little bit close together, and anything can happen. The day before the 1984 Jameson in Newcastle, Dennis Taylor and Willie Thorne were marooned in the Shetlands. The weather had closed in on them and no-one could be persuaded to fly them out. At last they found an operator who let them twist his arm

The circus arrives in town – the Matchroom Mob with entertainers Chas and Dave.

and agreed to fly them to Scotland. Landing on the northernmost tip, they ordered the first taxi they could find to drive them to Newcastle. Rumour has it that their fares cost them so much, they needed to reach the quarter-finals of the Jameson before they were out of the red.

And when the snooker circus does finally get to town, the hotel becomes the next disaster area.

There is Mark Wildman, posting his room key in the GPO letter box instead of the one for returned room keys. It happened during a recent World Doubles tournament.

There is Dennis Taylor, collecting his room key during the 1984 Yamaha event at Derby. Nothing remarkable about that, except that he has been **spotted by a breathless admirer**. As Dennis disappeared roomwards, the breathless admirer – a member of the ITV film crew who had broken his car key and could not get home – went over to reception and asked for a room.

'Well, not just a room,' he said. 'Can I have the room next to Dennis Taylor?'

The receptionist looked at the room chart and said that would be all right. The ITV man went contentedly to his room, already inventing phrases to go with his story – 'I kept bumping into Dennis Taylor, you know. He was in the next room as a matter of fact.' He opened the door, switched on the light... and wondered if he had arrived in the paint store by mistake. Paint tins were stacked all over the place. There was a bed, it was true – leant up against the wall. As far as rooms went, this one was definitely in an in-between state. Even the prospect of spending the night within feet of where Dennis Taylor slept, began to pall. Exit film man, mission *not* accomplished.

Finally, you can't keep a good man down. During the 1982 Pontins' Spring Festival Jimmy White arrived with one of those racing tips that are straight from the horse's mouth. This time, however, to general surprise, it came up trumps: Steve Cauthen's mount Far Too Much obliged at the very generous odds of 10 – 1 and Jimmy's delighted colleagues collected varying sums from the on-site bookmaker.

Later that evening the notice-board advising parents of awakening infants displayed a note saying 'Baby Crying in Chalet 10B'. Underneath, somebody had written **'Bookmaker crying in Reception'**.

SUPERLATIVE
SCORING FEATS

In the realm of billiards, it is more than a hundred years ago that the first 1000 break in public was made. Billy Mitchell scored it on 5 October 1882 in a match against William J. Peall at the Black Horse Hotel, Rathbone Place, London. His 1055 break included a sequence of 350 spot strokes.

Peall, an extraordinarily consistent player, made five four-figure breaks in four days, averaging 1500 per break, when he played Mitchell in November 1885 at the Royal Aquarium, London. On 4 November, he scored 1380 and 1709; on the 5th he got 1135; on the 6th he got 1257, and on the 7th his score was 1922.

Edward Diggle became the first player to keep an opponent from the table for a whole session after the rules barred spot strokes and made a push a foul stroke. Charles Dawson was the unlucky opponent, and the match was played at Brighton on 22 February 1902. It had been said that the outlawing of the push stroke would ruin Diggle's game.

Peall making another massive break of 2413 against Collins at the Royal Aquarium, 1886.

George Gray, the Australian, may have been the **first professional player to suffer a nervous breakdown** from competition pressure. In a way it is surprising that his unfortunate distinction was not achieved by Diggle, who was a

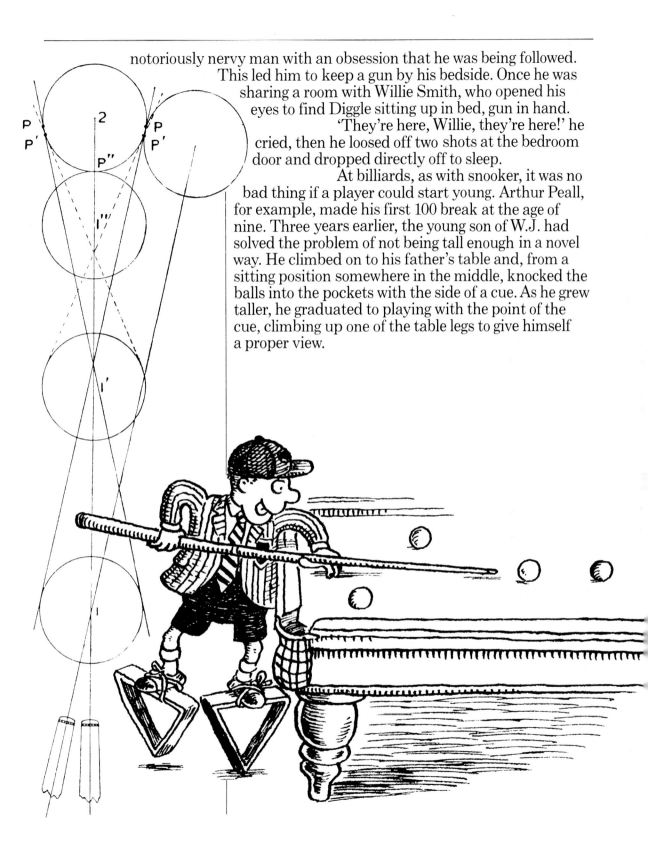

notoriously nervy man with an obsession that he was being followed. This led him to keep a gun by his bedside. Once he was sharing a room with Willie Smith, who opened his eyes to find Diggle sitting up in bed, gun in hand.

'They're here, Willie, they're here!' he cried, then he loosed off two shots at the bedroom door and dropped directly off to sleep.

At billiards, as with snooker, it was no bad thing if a player could start young. Arthur Peall, for example, made his first 100 break at the age of nine. Three years earlier, the young son of W.J. had solved the problem of not being tall enough in a novel way. He climbed on to his father's table and, from a sitting position somewhere in the middle, knocked the balls into the pockets with the side of a cue. As he grew taller, he graduated to playing with the point of the cue, climbing up one of the table legs to give himself a proper view.

Over, now, to snooker. In the old days, patience was even more of a virtue than it is today – and that went for spectators as well as players. The final of the current professional World Championship is fought out over the best of 35 frames, but spare a thought for the finalists (and the onlookers) at the 1952 finals, where the rules provided for a best of 145-frame match.

Only **a bizarre rule** prevented Fred Davis from receiving full credit for the first of his three wins over his brother Joe in competition play.

The 1948-49 Sunday Empire News Tournament at Leicester Square Hall had two handicaps. Each player received a handicap per frame but, in addition, there was a sealed handicap which said how many frames each player had to give his opponent.

Both Fred and Joe were off scratch in the frame handicap, and Fred proceeded to win the match by 36 frames to 35. When the sealed handicap envelope was opened, it revealed Fred was to concede two frames to Joe...which meant Joe won 37 – 36!

A report in the *Sheffield Telegraph* of 19 August 1912 describes the precocious feat of Jesse James, an employee at the Howard Billiard Saloon, Chapel Walk, Sheffield, who made a break of 70 while he was only 16 years old. *Billiards Monthly* commented:

'As the world record only stands at 72 the performance is a remarkable one, especially being made by a boy on a full-sized table.'

The record break by a professional player was then jointly held by John Roberts and James Harris at 73. Behind the scenes, however, the head marker at the Grand Hotel, Bristol made 83 in October 1909, and the manager of the Clarendon Hotel, Nottingham bettered this with a break of 87.

Best of all was the effort of the one-armed player Albert Williams, who on 14 May 1914 scored 74 in the billiard saloon attached to the Picture House in New Street, Birmingham. His break was made up of eight blacks, one blue, one green and ten reds.

According to *The Billiards Player*, the first snooker century was made in 1923 by Conrad Stanbury, the Canadian champion. Playing at the Palace Billiard Hall, Winnipeg, he scored 117.

Of course, it's not always what you do that is so important, it can be how old you are when you do it. Liverpool bookmaker Sid Lane, a keen supporter of the Pontins amateur and pro-am tournaments, compiled a century break during the 1983 Pontins Open. He was 70 years old at the time, and his previous century break had been in 1939.

Shortly after the outbreak of World War II the Sycamore Club and Canteen, a branch of the Amersham Free Church Institute, offered a special prize to high-scoring servicemen. They could win **100 cigarettes for a break of 100** at billiards, or 50 at snooker.

The first official maximum break was compiled by Joe Davis at the Leicester Square Hall on 22 January 1955, just a week before the Hall closed. However, he had to wait until March 1957 for ratification of the break by the Billiards Association and Control Club.

At that time the Billiards Association and Control Club rules did not

A challenge match in 1899 between the champion John Roberts and the young Yorkshireman Charles Dawson.

Steve Davis concentrates on some mental arithmetic.

make provision for an opponent to play again after a foul shot. However, Davis and his fellow-professionals did allow it. Impasse. Davis had to appeal several times before the ruling body relented and the first maximum was ratified – more than two years after it was made.

Willie Thorne is snooker's champion 'maximum' break maker, with more than 30 to his credit. He must also be the only player to have **scored a maximum with both legs in plaster!**

In 1982 he was involved in a go-karting accident, but this did not stop him from playing at his club in Leicester, with the aid of crutches. And there, with many a hop, step and jump, he compiled an amazing 147.

Appearing in his first World Championship, in 1979, Kirk Stevens had the chance to compile a championship record break on the opening day – until jumpy nerves took over. In his match with Graham Miles, Stevens had put together a 136 break and just needed an easy black for a new record of 143. He paused, took a deep breath – and missed. Compensation came in the 1984 Benson & Hedges Masters when he compiled one of the sport's rare televised 'maximums'.

Steve Davis, as everyone knows, registered the first televised 'maximum' during the 1982 Lada Classic at Oldham. But seasoned campaigner John Spencer could well have beaten him to it. Snooker writer and commentator Clive Everton was there. He recalls:

'The first 147 to be made in tournament play was at the Holsten Lager tournament in Slough in 1979. The event was being covered by Thames Television, but they had not managed to get the other TV companies to agree to network the programme. Because of this, they decided they could not afford two full crews, and so they did not have the manpower to cover every ball of every frame. Instead, they worked out a plan to cover certain frames only. Off the crew went for a meal break, and, of course, that was when John Spencer scored his record-setting 147. So there we were. The TV company had not filmed it. There was a highlights programme going out that night. **And I'm the commentator!'**

Willie Thorne enjoys a few moments of relaxation away from the table.

Willie Thorne had better luck at the 1985 Coral UK Open, when he scored a championship record break of 140 and had it filmed partly through chance and partly through his own persistence.

The Granada TV cameras were at the tournament, filming for a documentary on Thorne's opponent, Paddy Browne, and they decided to cover his important match against Thorne. When

Willie got to 127, with just the pink and black remaining, the camera ran out of film.

'Would you like me to wait?' asked Willie.

'Yes', replied the producer.

So Willie, obliging as ever, stood about while new film was loaded, then got down again and potted the last two balls.

One of snooker's **most out-of-place maximums** was registered in 1979 by the Australian amateur Leon Heywood. For his match with Graham Miles at the City Tatts Club in Sydney, Heywood was given a handicap of 21. With this

The 'magic' glasses failed to bring back the big breaks for Ray Reardon.

already under his belt, he went on to compile a 147 break and won the frame 168 – 0.

The record for the highest continuous snooker break is held by Alex Higgins. After losing 11 – 8 to Ray Reardon in a challenge match in 1981, the two players agreed to play out the 'dead' frames. Higgins cleared up with a 130 break. He then broke first in the next frame, fluked a red and proceeded to put together a 141 break, making a total of 271 without his opponent going to the table.

In terms of single frame scoring, is there anything better than 147? Yes, there most certainly is, and Higgins is again the man at the centre of the action.

The maximum will always be 147, but once in a very very blue moon a player gets a chance to go a little bit better. If there is a foul, when several reds are on the table, in theory the free ball makes it possible to clear the table and register an even higher score. This happened to Higgins one evening at Leicester YMCA. In play against Willie Thorne, he was awarded a free ball; he had four reds left, and could have hit a 149. Unfortunately, he **did not twig that the chance was on,** and let it go. Later he said: 'I was playing on one side of the table, and stayed there. It was easier than going round the other side. If I *had* gone round the other side...'

Makes you twitch, doesn't it?

More open-ended drama from Sydney, Australia, where Willie Fong and Lucky Hamlin set a bizarre record in 1985, playing continuous snooker for 187 hours 19 minutes, and beating the old record by eight minutes. Their record-breaking attempt took place at the Bondi Hotel, and raised money for a local charity.

This recent claim has been made for snooker's lowest score. Player 1 pots all the reds in one shot, then goes in off (4 – 0). Player 2 pots the yellow (6 – 0) but misses the green. Player 1 then pots the colours but misses the black. His opponent cannot get back to the table.

Final score: 18 – 6. Aggregate: 24.

Finally, tense news from Ireland where the *Daily Mirror* reported that Jimmy White had beaten Dennis Taylor 5 – 5 in the 1983 Irish Masters.

Well done, the both of youse!

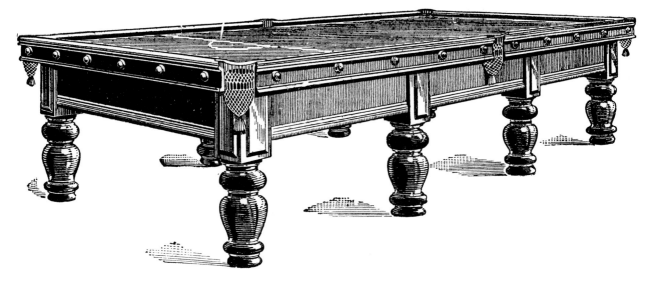

NIGHTS
BEST FORGOTTEN:
A BIZARRE
RECORD

BRIEFEST-EVER SESSION

Two old professionals arrived in Yarmouth to play an exhibition. Both were so drunk they could hardly stand up, but at last the harassed promoter managed to line them up beside him while he did the introductions. When play began, the first old pro got down, missed the reds altogether and almost fell over.

Harassed promoter: 'There will now be an interval.'

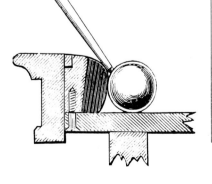

CUEITUS INTERRUPTUS

John Pulman was playing a match in the Chevron Hotel, Sydney. He was preparing to play an important shot when a message came over the public address:

'Mr John Smith. Wanted in the Foyer. Mr John Smith. Wanted in the foyer.'

Pulman hesitated. When silence resumed, he played the shot, but perhaps a shade too soon because he missed it. He stood up, banged his cue on the floor and shouted:

'F*;!! Mr Smith! And f*;!! the foyer!'

MOST OVERPLANNED MANOEUVRE

Sometimes a player's mind sets off down a certain track, goes too far

and loses itself. Eddie Charlton found this happening to himself in the 1974 World Championship. He potted a red, then drew up a vast mental map of what he should be doing up to about ten shots ahead. He became so engrossed in his plan, when he got down again he potted another red instead of a colour.

The horribly embarrassed feeling you get after a boob of that magnitude would have been familiar to John Barrie, a professional who achieved his most absent-minded feat not long after the Second World War. He broke off with the yellow. If you think about it, that must be quite difficult to do.

THE BILLIARD MONTHLY

A Journal of
Interest and Value to Amateur
Billiard Players.

The address of
The Billiard Monthly

14, Cross St., Finsbury
E.C.

No. 25   November, 1912   1/6 per annum to any part of
the World. Single copies, 1d.

The
Somnambulist

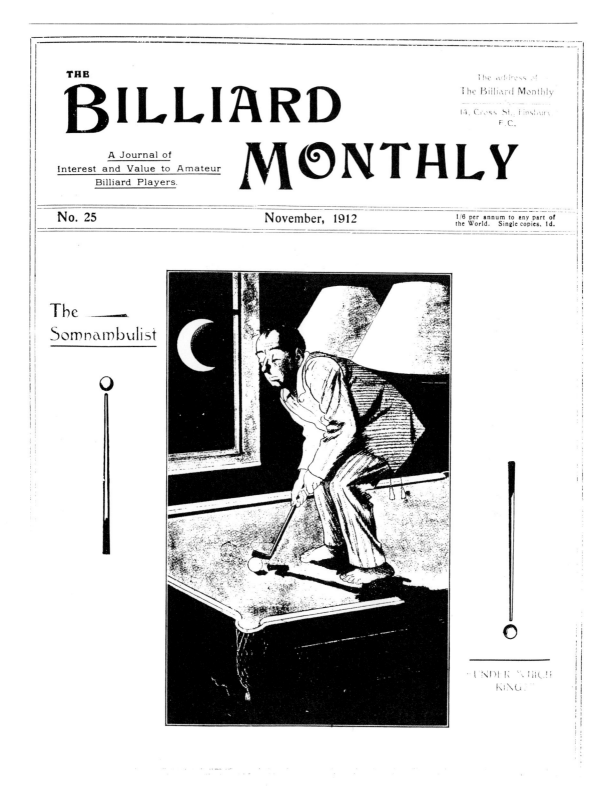

"UNDER WHICH
KING."

MOST UNHEARD-OF DEFEAT

In the Goya final of 1985, Jimmy White was leading Cliff Thorburn by 7 – 0 and had a lead of 74 points in the eighth frame, with four reds remaining. He lost the frame, then the match 12 – 10. In the history of professional snooker, this must rank as one of the worst on-the-table disasters ever suffered by a leading player.

BIGGEST TWITCHES

In his illustrious career Patsy Fagan suffered many an endless night – some of which were shown on television – while he fought his fear of playing shots with the rest.

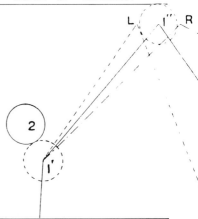

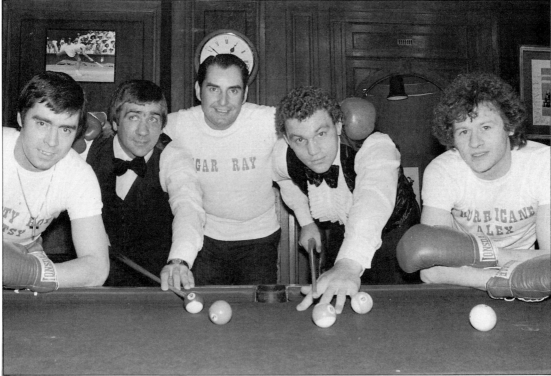

Patsy Fagan, Ray Reardon and Alex Higgins switch sports with heavyweight contenders Billy Aird and John L. Gardner in 1976.

Each time the shot came up, Patsy took the rest and put it on the table. He put his cue in position, lined up the shot…lined up the shot some more…then some more…went to hit it…and stuck. Poor Patsy, he could *not* let his arm go. Like golfers with the putting 'yips', he was suffering from that amazing mental seizure where the terrified brain paralyzes a movement of the body.

John Virgo had a similar problem for a while with under-the-cushion shots. This was when he was an amateur; he developed a terror for hitting cue-balls when they were under the cushion. John was not totally frozen, but he had to play the shot quickly. Walk up to it and hit it – bonk. He could not risk feathering the shot, or he would seize up.

Cushion shots were also the problem of an amateur from Hinckley called Ron Lamsden. He could *not* hit them. Ron, though, was philosophical about it. 'I had the same problem years ago when I was darting,' he explained. 'I couldn't let the arrer go!'

John Virgo during one of his cabaret routines.

SHRILLEST REF

No-one watching the 1981 World Team match between John Spencer (England) and Paddy Morgan (Australia), least of all the players, could understand why the game was suddenly interrupted by bells. Shrill, insistent bells which, moreover, seemed to come from somewhere very close to referee John Smyth. Was this some new change in the laws – perhaps an experimental time penalty – which no-one had told them about?

Of course not. It was an alarm clock going off in the referee's pocket. He had bought a new battery for it earlier in the day, loaded it in the clock, put the clock in his pocket and forgotten about it. Ah well, even referees can't win them all.

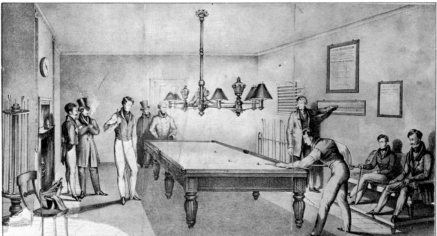

Spot the differences – three illustrations of The Billard Room used by leading manufacturers J. Thurston & Co.

ABROAD:
BIZARRE FEATS
FROM ACROSS
— THE —
WATER

SHORTEST TOUR OF INDIA (ANCIENT)

When John Roberts Jr was world professional billiards champion, he went on tour to India many times. On the first occasion he shipped out some tables with him, planning to sell them to wealthy customers.

Advised that the Maharajah of Jaipur was a keen sportsman, Roberts hired some elephants to transport a batch of samples to the Maharajah's palace. The great man said he would take half a dozen tables, and appointed Roberts as Court Billiards Player for life, granting him a salary of £500 a year plus his travelling expenses provided he spent one month a year at the palace.

Once he had got the taste for billiards, the Maharajah wanted to stage his own tournament. Roberts tried to explain that this would entail bringing eight players halfway across the world by boat, train and elephant, and would almost certainly be impossible to achieve. But the Maharajah would listen to no excuses; he wanted his tournament, and, money being evidently no object, that is what he got.

In the opening match Roberts played S.W. Stanley, a clever player with a rather edgy, temperamental character. Stanley played a safety shot, which let Roberts in near the red spot. The spot stroke being allowed in those days, Roberts happily potted the red about twenty times until he was suddenly interrupted by the Maharajah, who was clearly getting bored by this repetitious play. The royal host stepped down from his throne, picked up the balls and declared:

'We will have the next game. Roberts is the winner.'

Stanley was thus abruptly eliminated, having travelled thousands of miles and played one safety shot. Word has it that he never forgave Roberts and was never quite the same man again.

SHORTEST TOUR OF INDIA (MODERN)

Alex Higgins arrived in Bombay to find that an exhibition match had been arranged for him the same evening. It was hot and humid at the venue. Off came the tie. Drinks were hastily swallowed in the hope that they would have a cooling effect. Followed by more drinks. Off came the shirt. The heat grew worse.

As the evening wore on, Higgins began cheerfully to insult his opponents, then he grew curious about the dhotis that several of the men were wearing. What, he wanted to know, did an Indian wear underneath his dhoti? Instead of quietly asking someone, however, Higgins preferred to carry out some on-the-spot research, lifting a hem or two with the tip of his cue. Unfortunately, he was dealing with some very up-market Indians and they got very upper-crusty about the Irishman's experiments. Next morning, Higgins was on a plane home.

MOST SERPENTINE DRINKING PARTNER

After losing to Tony Knowles in the first round of the Belgian Classic in Ostend, Jimmy White ran into further difficulties back at his hotel. In the bar was a cabaret artiste who featured an enormous python in her act. One of White's entourage was able to persuade the lady to fetch her long pet and let it slither across the snooker player's shoulders. Taken literally aback by the python, White's response was quite unprintable.

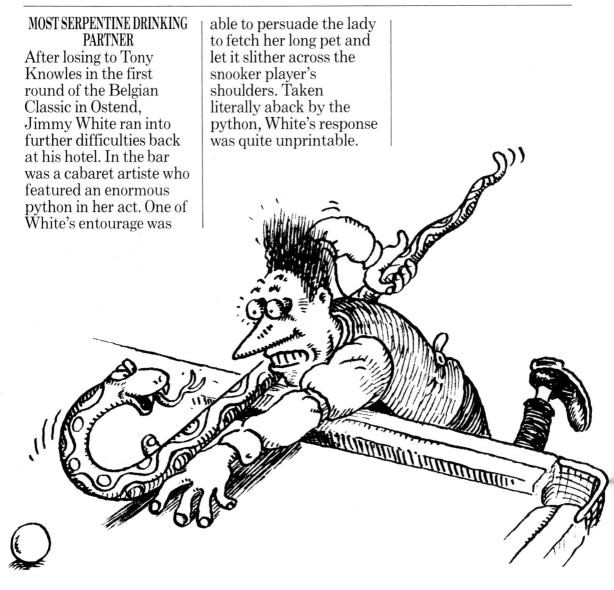

Colonial rule introduced billiards and snooker to some unlikely competitors.

The Illustrated London News *reports on play in Manila. 1858.*

WORST AWAY TRIP

Mohammed Lafir, the diminutive Sri Lankan who became world amateur billiards champion in 1973, would probably rank his journey to Malta in 1971 as one of his best-forgotten experiences. Still recovering from an illness, he arrived on the island to find that his luggage had gone to

Rome. Speaking little English he made the best of his circumstances but obviously had difficulty in reading labels; on the plane he had put mustard in his coffee.

Long before his missing luggage could be retrieved, Lafir was pressed into action at the Malta Hilton. Lacking a dress suit, he borrowed one belonging to Michael Ferreira. Lafir's weight was then down to about seven stone, whereas Ferreira weighed fifteen stone, so the fit was far from perfect. At least, though, he had his own cue, which must have been some consolation; using it, he won his first match, against David Sneddon, before going out 1423 – 790 to Mannie Francisco.

In 1974, at the World Amateur Snooker Championships in Dublin, Lafir had problems of a different nature. All the other players felt comfortable and warm; but Lafir was cold. Try as he might, he could not get warm. He wore a sweater under his dress shirt; it made no difference. Every time he played, a Calor Gas stove was put near him; he still shivered. He kept sending out for pots of coffee, and used the pot to try and warm his hands; poor chap, nothing would work for him.

Lafir, incidentally, had a bizarre introduction to the game. He learned to play billiards on the family dining table. The cue was a broomstick, the balls were toy marbles, the cloth was a sarong, and the cushions were provided by a cycle's inner tube.

WHITER THAN WHITE

In the departure lounge at Heathrow, on his way to the Canadian Open, Alex Higgins was spotted with a huge holdall.

'What have you got there?' he was asked.

'My washing,' he said. 'Toronto. They have the best laundry service in the world.'

NOISIEST CHAMPIONSHIP

Players arriving for the 1976 Canadian Open little realized what a farce they were letting themselves in for. In those days the event was staged at the National Exhibition Centre in Toronto. Playing conditions were fairly tough at the best of times, because the snooker had to take its place beside other shows or exhibitions: behind the partitions other spectators might be watching a fashion show, for instance; tannoys would send out distracting messages, and the air-conditioning unit (it was high summer) made a terrible racket.

This particular year there had been a mix-up over the bookings. The snooker players were given two choices: play the tournament in a circus tent, or not at all; the tent was the only place left. They agreed to play, and were shown the tent which was sited next to the circus to which it belonged; on the other side was a concert auditorium.

The temperature was in the nineties, with high humidity. The noise from the circus was deafening enough, without the added input of assorted bands and orchestras. That was not all. As a special treat, every hour on the hour, a man was fired from a gun.

Then Nature had her say. A cloudburst of epic proportions flooded the tent, and when play resumed everyone was walking round the tables on duckboards. Anyone who was there, not surprisingly, speaks of it still.

UNLIKELIEST ARAB

Alex Higgins had been playing in one of the Gulf States, and he was due to fly to Sydney on a connecting flight from Bahrain. He knew that John Virgo, Jimmy White & Co would be on the incoming plane, so he dressed up as an Arab sheikh, complete with dark glasses, and went into the departure lounge. Spotting his victims, he went over to them and started nudging them. They were beginning to wonder what this strange robed creature wanted from them when – hey presto! Higgins whips off the shades and all is revealed.

Two more unlikely Arabs – Terry Griffiths (left) and Steve Davis on their return from Dubai.

CLUBROOM
CALAMITIES

Fire, Explosion, Lightning and Earthquake, Aircraft and Aerial Devices, Malicious Persons or Vandals, Impact by Road or Rail Vehicles, Horses or Cattle... All these and more can – to borrow the language of the insurance companies – cause serious damage to snooker tables.

The Residency at Lucknow after the attack in 1857.

The Buffalo Club, Kimberley, 1900.

The accompanying photographs, from the Indian Mutiny and the Boer War, give only a mild impression of the **terminal devastation** inflicted on billiard and snooker tables in the last century and a half from one source alone – war. As for the effect on the players present at the time, the following letter gives an indication of what happens to their mental state.

It was written in June 1941 to the Editor of *The Billiard Player*. This, readers will recall, was at the height of the Blitz. It states:

'I am told that Joe Davis once potted all the snooker balls except one red in one visit to the table, but I can go one better than that, for the other night I potted all the balls with one stroke. Yes, sir – it's true. I had just made the opening stroke when bang went a large high explosive right outside our station. All the balls immediately got the wind up and dived into the pockets for safety.

'Do I get a proficiency break certificate?'

The Editor was clearly a man accustomed to the sad spectacle of a snooker player deranged by the hazards of war. He replied, not 'Lock this man up' but 'We should like notice of that question.'

The Royal Navy, meanwhile, were having their own problems. In the years between the wars, battleships such as HMS *Nelson* were fitted with various modern amenities including billiard tables. An excellent idea, though on the high seas (where cunning devices such as those shown in 'Bizarre Venues' were not available) it was found necessary to improvise. Instead of having snooker balls flying calamitously all over the place, the sailors invented a new game – snooker without cues. *The Billiard Player* reported:

'The coloured balls were put on their respective spots, each officer taking a ball as in life pool. Each officer placed his ball on its appropriate spot, and held it there until the order was given to 'leave go'. Bets having been made beforehand, the first ball to run into a pocket scooped the pool.'

The Chief Petty Officers' Billiard Room on HMS Nelson, 1928.

Most civilized. And not a word about sinking tables or players being lashed by spray from the sea outside. No, you have to go to Manchester if you want a story about **snooker in the rain**.

In 1973, rain stopped play in the World Championships. Fred Davis was playing Alex Higgins in a quarter-final match when Fred suddenly felt an unfamiliar drop of wetness. Incredulous, he looked up and saw that rain was actually getting in through a hole in the roof. The covers were hastily put on and play was suspended until the hole had been plugged.

For the professional player, clubroom calamities begin with the table itself. If that is not up to the mark, he will be hard-pressed to think that the evening will be anything other than calamitous. Over the years, the pros have developed a private stock of insults which they mutter to each other and to the organizers. Here, for instance, is John Pulman, registering dismay in the face of dodgy equipment:

'You need a map from the AA to play on this table.' And:

'The only thing these cushions are doing is stopping the balls from falling on the floor.'

He also had a nice line in derision for opponents he regarded as below-par. For instance:

'The last time he won a match, a star appeared in the East.' And, faced with a slow player:

'If you played him in a week's match, it would take a fortnight.'

Ray Reardon, too, has a good capacity for describing shortcomings. Of a table with easy pockets:

'When you were walking past the middle pocket, you had to be careful you didn't fall into it.' And, poetically, when these were on the tight side:

John Virgo (left) and Ray Reardon – two of the great entertainers.

'The pockets were like mouse's ears.'

Clive Everton recalls a number of calamities which happened in the early years of televised snooker:

'Before they had the present system of television lighting, there were two or three occasions when a **bulb exploded and crashed down on the table**, burning the cloth or just missing a player. At the Park Drive final in 1971 or '72, they were playing with a new design of table which had formica cushion rails. Under the extremely hot television lights, these rails got so hot they started to curl up.

'It wasn't so good for the players, either. If they had to play a shot under the cushion, they had to nip in very quickly and hit it – or they got their hand burnt!'

Returning to our first paragraph, and the kind of calamity that would interest an insurance company, St Helen's Snooker Club had an unlucky break in 1982. The day after the club opened, the entire premises were burned to the ground, **destroying all fifteen new tables.**

On the subject of fire, this slightly disturbing notice appeared on the wall of a snooker hall in Morden, Surrey. It said:

' FIRE EXIT AT REAR OF HALL. MEMBERS ONLY.'

Then there was the Case of the Snooker Widow. This lady, apparently affronted by the hours her husband spent at his snooker club in Maidstone, stormed in there one evening and **slashed the baize on thirteen tables.** A witness commented:

'It is definitely an unusual way to stop someone playing.'

Finally, a very strange and calamitous tale from pre-war Germany. A man called Georg Lanzer was playing billiards with a friend in a room over a cafe in Berlin. He experimented with a forcing shot and the ball left the table and disappeared through the open window. Both men went down into the alley next to the cafe to look for the ball. There was no sign of the ball, but smoke was issuing in clouds from the ground-floor window of a cottage on the opposite side of the alley. They knocked on the door but there was no reply. They heard a cat yowling and decided to do something, so they climbed in through the window and were just in time to rescue the cat from the burning room.

Railwaymen take a break between shifts.

It seems that the ball had shot in through the open window, and hit the cat which had been asleep on a chair. The cat had taken a wild leap, clawed at a table cloth, upset a spirit lamp and started a fire. The ball later came to light in the corner of the room.

Georg Lanzer had done well. He had saved the cat, and then he had put out the fire. Instead of being congratulated by the returning owner, however, he and his friend **scared her, literally, to death.** The elderly woman, faced by two smoke-grimed men in her own house, screamed 'Burglars!' and dropped down dead.

The police were sent for, and the alley filled with excited people. Both men were arrested. Medical evidence then proved that the woman had died from a heart attack, and the men were cleared.

A week later, a distressed young woman went to the police. The deceased woman was her aunt, a wealthy woman who had not only a great deal of money but also many nephews and nieces. Her will stated that her estate should be equally divided.

The young woman told the police that she was engaged to the son of a wealthy family who had withheld their consent to the marriage unless the girl could produce a substantial sum of money. She had consulted her aunt who said:

'As you are my favourite, I will alter my will so that your romance may be realized. You will have many thousands of marks. Go away and arrange your marriage.'

Her story was ratified by the lawyer who had made an appointment to see the aunt the day after her death. But, the law being the law, nothing could be done to alter the will and the young woman's fiancé withdrew his proposal.

As Georg Lanzer remarked to his friend: 'He couldn't have been a billiards player!'

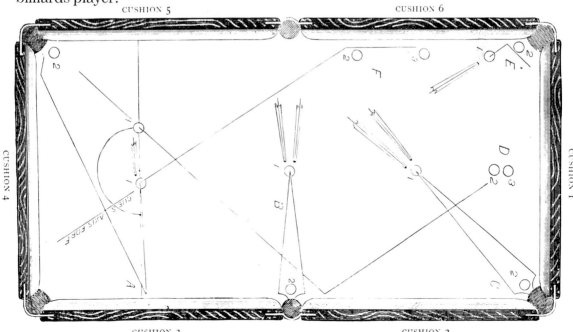

87

THE LONG UPHILL STRUGGLE OF THE LADY PLAYER

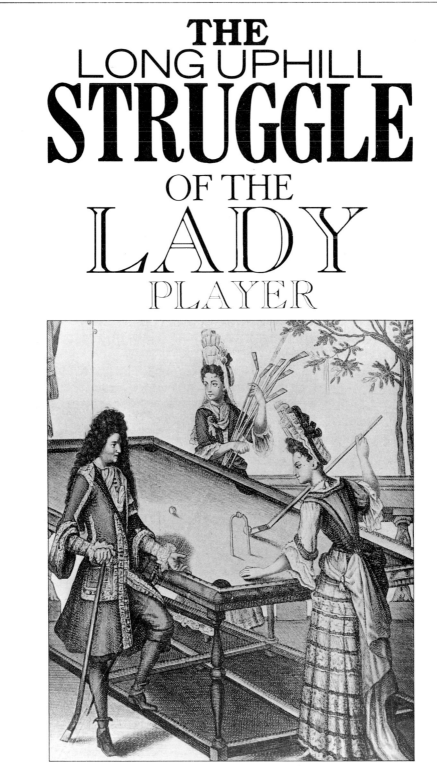

A battle of the sexes in the late 17th century.

Woman's lot in the snooker game has always been hard. Back in 1576, Mary Queen of Scots complained to Queen Elizabeth I that she was being subjected to severe cruelty. Not only was she locked up in Fotheringay Castle, they would not let her have her billiard table.

Even in our supposedly more enlightened times, discrimination abounds. In June 1983, a Tory woman barrister was barred from her local Conservative Club because of a row over women playing snooker. Dawn Oakes, aged 24, wrote to Mrs Thatcher about it, whereupon she received a letter from the Association of Tory Clubs saying that Dawn's club, St Annes, was one of only two in the country where women were banned.

The Secretary of the St Annes club said: 'We have just paid out £2,000 for a new set of tables, and I dread to think what might happen if we let women loose on them.'

In May 1985, Chris Cornish turned up to play for Rugby Snooker Centre against Lutterworth. When the opposition saw that Chris was a woman, they refused to play against her.

'Right,' said Chris's team-mates, 'no match.' And they all walked out. Soon after this incident it was established that three other clubs in the local snooker league had barred women players. Not, they claimed, because they did not want women getting in on a male-dominated sport. League Secretary Gordon Coulthard had another explanation:

'The objections put forward are that women's hand cream makes the balls unplayable, and their diamond rings rip the cloth.'

Fortunately, the game every so often produces a woman player who is so outstanding that her presence cannot be ignored. Mandy Fisher is the current example, able to play as well as the top amateur men, something which has not happened before.

Mandy Fisher tries her hand on a circular table.

In the 1940s and '50s the big name belonged to Joyce Gardner, who was much respected by her male professional colleagues. Joyce was the first woman to commentate on snooker for the BBC, and she also holds the unique record of being the first snooker player, male or female, to have their portrait hung in the Royal Academy.

In more recent times the crown passed to Vera Selby. She did not start playing snooker until she was 37. But within two years she won her first national title and then, in 1981, she won the World Championship. In recognition her home city of Newcastle-upon-Tyne made her their Sports Council's Personality of the Year.

Finally, the following report has reached us, sent in by two very ambitious young ladies aged twelve and thirteen, Helen Bacon and Emily Lomax, from Barby, near Rugby. Entitled 'Cornered, At The Hofmeister', it reveals a bright new angle on the future of the game.

CORNERED, AT THE HOFMEISTER

The electric atmosphere of a professional tournament was pressing around us – Steve Davis hunters! We were waiting just outside the dressing rooms. We had befriended a commissionnaire called Denis (not Taylor!!!) who had arranged that if Steve Davis went to the hospitality room for a drink after his interviews we would be able to see him (Steve not Dennis!!!) alone! To Steve we were just ordinary fans, but to others, especially ourselves, we were different!

Steve Davis, well protected from unauthorised visitors.

From the sub-tropically heated dressing room (you see we know all about this sort of thing!) out stepped Steve! We had been waiting for this for so long, but he only had time to say hello to us before he was whisked off upstairs into the crowd to sign autographs for all the ordinary fans. All was not lost, we followed Steve up the stairs, then we realized we were going to have to join the ten-mile-long queue of autograph hunters and wait!

We were prepared! For a whole year we had been planning this day and it wasn't going to go wrong now!

PLAN C INTO ACTION!

(Tony Knowles had ruined plan A!)

This was to wait until last to get Steve's autograph, therefore missing, accidentally of course, the last train back to Rugby station. (If this plan failed, we had other plans through to X.)

Having decided this we turned around and...came face to face with Tony Meo, who was stumbling as we had almost knocked him down the stairs!!!

Instead of doing what any normal person would have done, step aside and apologize hurriedly in a rather embarrassed voice, we realized this was our big chance, and we took it!!!

He was holding a drink, a cue case, his tuxedo on a hanger and a few other things, and was rather laden down.

We, being our usual mad selves, rushed in and said: 'Please could you sign this, Tony.' People around us stared in shock and horror and moved to get a better view.

Emily, seeing his arms were rather full, said ''ere, I'll hold this,' taking his glass of rather nondescript, green liquid, the horrific, pungent aroma smacking her around the face. He looked slightly taken aback (understatement of the year) but nevertheless, with a smiling face he signed his autographs, although we have our suspicions about one of them as he signed it with his right hand!

After that we got in the queue for autographs. Steve Davis, our hero and the poor, victimized Tony Meo looked at us in shock horror (as if to say, 'Oh God, not those two again!')

Then we told them our ear-splitting, heart-rending, brain-reeling news... We are training to become professional Lady Snooker Refs!!!!!!

Tony Meo, the gentleman-but security men might query what he was carrying in his cue case.

The first lady referee. Ruth Harrison takes charge of a match between Willie Smith (right) and

Sidney Smith in 1932.

IN THE SNOOKER ROOM: BIZARRE VARIANTS

THE ANTI-SNOOKER LOBBY

If Willie Smith had had his way, snooker would never have got off the ground. Willie, twice winner of the World Professional Billiards Championship, said he only played it because it was currently more popular than billiards.

'But,' he warned darkly, 'people will never stand for it.'

Two years before his death in 1982 he was asked whether his views on snooker had changed, given that the game was now so successful. Willie was unrepentant.

'They should change the rules,' he replied, 'all of them.'

ORIGINAL ORIGINS

Most readers will be familiar with the origin of the term 'snooker'. It was first used to describe raw cadets at Woolwich Academy and was then extended by officers of the Devonshire Regiment serving in India to mean someone who played the new game they had invented to help pass the long afternoons during the rainy season.

Many, however, will be less familiar with the origin of the word 'billiards'. The Australian champion George Gray had a particularly interesting account, which emerged in the course of an interview he was giving.

'Yes,' said Gray, 'I used to practise losing hazards into a guarded top pocket without touching a peg placed against one of the shoulders. I mastered it in the end, but it wasn't easy and sometimes I used to bless – or otherwise – the very name of Kew.'

'Kew?' asked the interviewer.

'Yes, the man who invented billiards,' explained Gray. 'Don't you remember William Kew? He lived in the middle of the sixteenth century and was a pawnbroker. When trade was slack, he used to take down the three balls of his sign and push them about the counter with a yard measure into boxes fixed at the sides. In time the idea of a fenced table with pockets suggested itself and hence the game of bill-yards – from "William" and the "yard measure" he used. "Cue", of course, is only another spelling of his surname and "cannons" are so called because it was a clergyman who invented them.'

Well, that should settle a few arguments.

CORK POOL AND CORONATION CORK POOL BILLIARDS

Messrs Burroughes and Watts were also responsible for devising these rules for two other fascinating variants. One winter evening, you may like to give them a go.

CORK POOL

This popular game is played by any number of players, with two balls, a red and a white. A cork is placed on the centre spot of the table, and on this the pool agreed upon is put; the red is placed on the billiard spot, and the first person who succeeds in making a cannon from the red to the cork, striking a cushion previous to striking the cork, receives the whole pool.

1. At the commencement of the game the red ball is placed on the billiard spot, and the cork with the pool agreed on in the centre of the table.
2. The order of play is determined by giving out the pool balls in rotation from a basket, or by numbered counters.
3. The first player plays from baulk with the white ball, and each succeeding player from where the white stops; if it is pocketed the next player plays from the baulk.
4. Each player has only one stoke according to his rotation.
5. Any player making a cannon receives the whole pool.
6. A cannon can only be made by striking the red first, then a cushion, and lastly the cork.
7. Should any player miss the red, pocket same, touch the cork, make a cannon on to it without first striking a cushion, play out of turn, or pocket his own white ball, he must pay the same stake as at starting, and add it to that already on the cork.
N.B. The game is frequently played in private circles with a penalty only for knocking down the cork without striking the red ball and cushion.

CORONATION CORK POOL BILLIARDS

1. This game is played by two or more players, either all against all, or in partnership. The points are 63 or 126 up, including a number.
2. The three billiard balls are used, a special red and white cork, and 16 numbers.
3. When commencing the game, the spot ball is placed on the right-hand spot of baulk line; the plain on the left; the cork on the middle spot and the red on the billiard spot.
4. The sixteen numbers in a basket are shaken up and given out, one to each player, first for rotation (lowest first) and then secretly for play.
5. A player choosing a ball must, when in hand, play always from his own spot.
6. After choosing a ball, the player continues with the same, if an even number of players; but if an odd number are playing, with the alternate ball.
7. The baulk line is protection.
8. The game scores as at billiards, the cork counting ten points after striking a ball but it is of no consequence which ball knocks the cork down.
9. If the striker's ball knocks the cork down without hitting a ball, he loses eleven

The sons of Louis XIV enjoy a military variant.

points off his score. Should he, after striking the cork first, hit a ball, he only loses ten points.

10. Running a coup, giving a miss, or a ball going off the table counts against the player, and the penalty is taken off his score; but a player can give an intentional miss, or run a coup, to suit his own secret number.

11. A player must make the exact score (63 or 126) including his secret number. Going over his number he loses the game, if two playing or partners; but if all against all the game continues until a winner is declared.

DOTTED LINES MARK SKYLIGHT 12 FT SQ

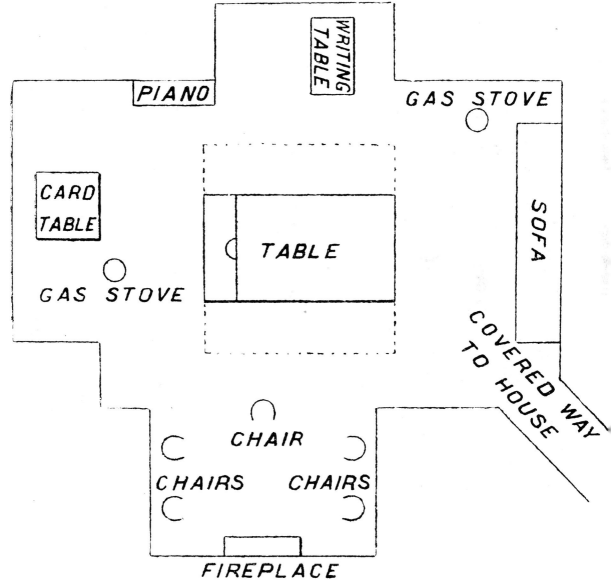

12. The cork is replaced where it falls, red part downwards, but if in any way it is impeded by cushion, ball, or knocked off the table, it is replaced on its own spot.

13. If the cork is jammed in any way between table and cushions, leans against a ball or cushion, or is in any way not lying perfectly flat on the table, it is considered up, and the striker does not count the ten points; but the cork, if it cannot be put up, is placed on its own spot. If the cork is knocked down and stands up again it is considered up, and remains where it stands, and the player does not count the ten points.

14. If any ball or the cork is impeding a striker in placing his ball on his proper spot, they are moved to their respective spots.

15. If the red cannot be spotted, the ball or cork occupying the spot is moved as per Rule 14, and if the ball is the striker's, he plays from his own spot.

16. If the striker is in hand, and his spot is occupied by the opponent's ball, that ball is placed on its own spot, and is not playable as per Rule 7.

17. If the striker plays with the ball, and the error is discovered by the opponent before the next stroke, the score does not count, but the balls and cork are placed on their respective spots, and it is left to the opponent to say which player breaks the balls.

18. The push and spot strokes are not barred, and the balls if touching are still playable.

19. Foul strokes are: playing from the wrong spot; touching a ball, except when in hand; playing out of turn; striking a ball more than once; playing before the balls have become stationary; lifting both feet from off the floor; disturbing the cork in any other way than the proper manner. The penalty is, the striker cannot score.

20. A player may demand that an opponent stand a fair distance out of the line of sight of cork or ball, whilst in the act of aiming.

SNOOKER-GOLF

Here is a golf-type game, which any number up to four can play at the same time. This is how *The Billiard Player* described the rules in its August 1939 issue:

'Each player has a pair of snooker colours, 1 red and white, 2 green and yellow, 3 blue and brown, 4 black and pink. In each instance the first named colour is the cue-ball and the second is the object ball. The top left-hand pocket is Hole No. 1 and so round the table, finishing left-hand middle. First round the course wins.

Each player has one stroke at a time unless he gets his correct pocket, in which case the object ball is spotted on the centre and he plays the cue ball from its lie. The object is to pot into the next pocket or play an approach shot which will make this task simple next time – if someone does not interfere.

One other rule must be applied. When a player has achieved his fifth hole the object ball is spotted on the red spot – not the centre for his approach to the sixth hole.

The skill and difficulty of the game arises in the fact that the player must first strike his object ball with his cue ball before he can pot his own or make either of his colours incommode an opponent. Failure to do this does not permit him to disturb the lie of the rest of the field. If there is a possibility of this, the other balls must be marked before he makes his stroke.

Penalty is loss of a pocket. You will see the merit in this when, if an opponent is going for the sixth hole and others are behind, a concerted effort to keep his object ball from having a clear run to that pocket forces him to foul and so keeps the game alive, as he then has to go for No. 5 again. The same penalty is enforced for in-offs, potting any other player's cue-ball in any pocket, or any object ball in a wrong pocket – potted in the right one, the owner scores – and for any of the usual foul strokes of the table.

After a foul the player loses his turn and a pocket, his colours are taken from the table, and he plays his next shot from the original centre spot position.

Try the game and it will soon simplify itself as to the rules, although it may be a long time before you become good at it. It is simply 'clock-putting' with rivals interfering – by getting one or the other of their colours in the line of the pocket – but for development of a sense of strength, an appreciation of angles, and two or even three-cushion doubles, the game is very instructive indeed.'

SKILL POOL

Here is a game, christened Skill Pool, which in 1909 was sponsored by Burroughes and Watts at their billiard saloon in Soho Square, London. The rules were described as follows:

'The player commencing the game places the white ball anywhere in the D, and plays for a cannon off the red ball on to any coloured ball. Two points are scored for the cannon, and should the red be pocketed when a cannon is made, two more may be added. The break is continued by playing from the position the balls are in, for a winning or losing hazard, or both, off the coloured ball first struck when the cannon was made.

'After scoring off a coloured ball, the break is continued by playing a cannon off the red ball from the position in which the balls are left, and then as before. Provided the cannon is made, any hazard made in the same stroke is credited to the striker in addition to the cannon score.'

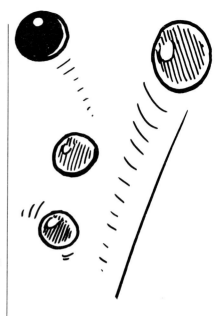

The art of Skill Pool as described by The Illustrated Sporting and Dramatic News *in 1909.*

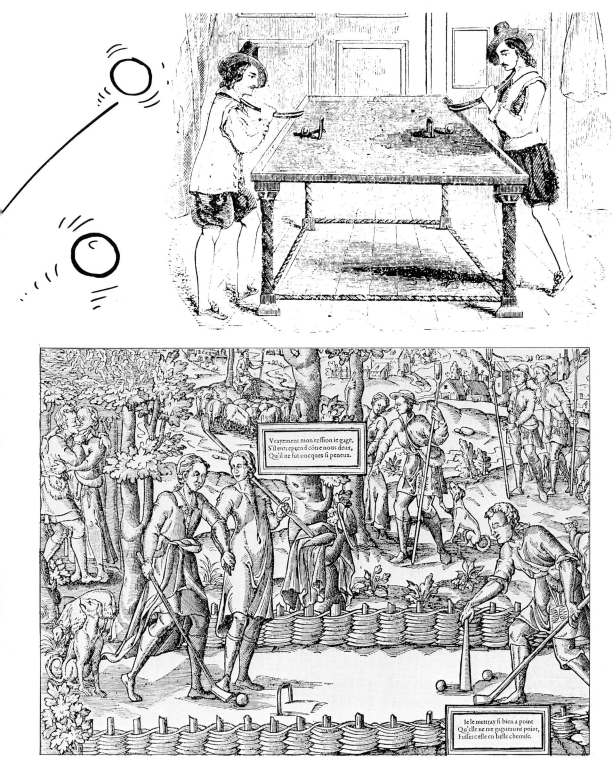

A version of billiards played outdoors by the French in the 16th century.

Melbourne Inman demonstrates his game of Banking to Joe Davis (centre) and Tom Newman.

BANKING

Not so easy to emulate is this game, devised in 1930 and in the photograph being promoted by Melbourne Inman. It was played with standard balls and cues but the holes, bunkers and other hazards around the nine-hole course were obviously tailor-made.

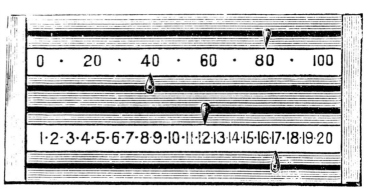

SNOOKER PLUS

This was devised by Joe Davis and launched in 1959 at Burroughes Hall. Snooker Plus is played with two extra balls: an orange, worth eight points, and a purple, worth ten points. The new maximum was increased from 147 to 210 and, although Davis compiled the first century at the new game, the highest recorded Snooker Plus break was one of 156 by Jackie Rea.

I AM A BILLIARD TABLE

At least that was what the costumier Harrison evidently thought. He won first prize at Olympia in 1894 with a billiard table costume. A shade formed the headpiece; the arms and legs were dressed to look like the legs of the table. The front showed the cloth of the table, and the cue, rest, balls and pockets were all depicted, according to one report, 'in a realistic manner'.

Sounds totally potty to us.

James Stuart (centre), 'The Old Pretender', playing billiards at Versailles.

TRICKY STUFF

Joyce Gardner strings off for break before her match with Sidney Smith.

Most people would say that Joe Davis, in his day, could do more things with a set of snooker balls than anyone else. That would be to ignore the claims of Tommy Leng, who owned a number of billiard halls and who performed perhaps the most unusual trick of all.

Assisted by Joyce Gardner, he was blindfolded with adhesive plaster over both eyes, and by wads of cotton wool and towels. The balls were then placed on the table in all the wrong positions, with one or two colours in the pack. Leng's trick was to move the balls until they were all on their right spots.

Leng claimed that he studied mental telepathy. He was reported to have said: 'In a hushed hall I can hear the audience "screaming" out the colours of the balls in my hands and the spot at which I am standing.' The effort was so great that once he nearly blacked out during his performance.

Trick shots are, of course, an all-important part of snooker exhibition matches. One man who went rather too far was Raymond Priestly, an Australian, whose 'shot of a lifetime' proved to be his last.

In Melbourne in 1979 he set himself up for the **supreme Down Under shot,** suspended by his feet from the rafters. Cue in hand, he went to play the shot, slipped and fell, breaking his neck. He was killed instantly.

We presume he had already obtained a special dispensation from the rule that requires a player to have one foot on the ground.

Frank Ives relied on a mysterious reservoir of amazing strength for his most famous claim – that he could hit a billiard ball with a cue harder than any man in the world. As *Pearson's Weekly* reported in October 1896, not even champion boxers could outdo him:

'Corbett, Fitzsimmons, Sandow, and other athletes and strong men have competed with him, but he has not been beaten yet. One quick, sharp blow with his cue and the ball flies round the table, striking eleven cushions. Fitzsimmons who strikes a blow that has been compared to a horse's kick, can barely touch nine cushions, while Corbett, whose blows are equally unpleasant, cannot strike more than eight.

Leon Goffart, the Belgian Billiardist.

Generally acknowledged to be the greatest Trick=shot Player living

I F not well known to Englishmen, the name of Goffart, the Belgian Wizard of th

'There is no trick in Ives's method of hitting the ball; he merely strikes it squarely in the centre. Men who are in every way superior to him in strength, if shown exactly where to hit the ball, and if they strike it with all the force they possess, cannot come within a dozen feet of his record. He has consulted eminent physicians on the subject, but they gave him little satisfaction, except to say that his profession had led to the development of muscles which prize fighters and strong men do not use.

'As Ives cannot settle the question to his own satisfaction he has taken steps to enlighten others after his death. In his will, after disposing of his property – £60,000 – he orders that his **right arm be severed from his body** and sent to

Dennis Taylor lines up one of his 'party pieces'.

his physician for dissection. The real secret, he thinks, will then be discovered. The rest of his body he desires to be cremated.'

The turn of the century was also the era of Miss May Kaarlus, described in a 1901 article as 'a Billiard Marvel who Defies the Male Champions'. Miss Kaarlus was very much the *protegée* of her father, Professor Kaarlus, a Belgian expert in the science of the game.

Several years previously, the Professor had been stung by a newspaper columnist who asserted that women could do anything except play billiards. Professor Kaarlus resolved to prove the journalist wrong, and selected his daughter May as his model. Years of strict training followed and then, soon after her sixteenth

A tricky shot for comedian Norman Collier, a popular performer in pro-celebrity matches.

Joe Davis demonstrates his skills.

Fred Hall shows how to pocket fourteen balls with one shot.

birthday, May Kaarlus made a resounding début at Maurice Daly's Academy in New York.

She seemed to have all the shots of the best players of the day, and although it was not part of her father's plans that she should compete against the top men at their own kind of game, he proposed instead a novel form of competition. He drew up a repertoire of a hundred trick shots, and announced that May would take on any challenger over the full distance. A record would be kept of the number of attempts needed to make each shot, and the player who made the hundred with the smallest total of attempts would be the winner.

The World of Billiards was most impressed by Miss Kaarlus, and their reporter was clearly won over by her charm:

'Miss Kaarlus is modest, and the perfection of physical grace and strength. Her attention to athletic training is incessant, and is indispensable to her wonderful success in close draw, wing, and follow-shots. In many of her amazing round-the-table performances the most perfect muscular development is needed to drive the elusive ivory spheres through the strange figures that they must describe.'

A tricky customer, indeed.

One of the favourite tricks is the machine-gun shot, where one ball is sent rolling slowly towards the pocket and the others are fired in so quickly that the cue-ball is the last to drop. One night in Truro, Cornish referee Walter James

crouched behind the pocket, watching intently as Joe Davis rattled in his machine-gun salvo.

As the balls went into the pocket, they piled up on top of one another, forming a kind of chute. The last-but-one ball zoomed straight at the pocket, then hit the chute and careered over the top – and **knocked out the referee's front teeth.**

Terry Griffiths was in Northern Ireland one night, giving an exhibition which finished with a group of trick shots. He was explaining to the audience what he planned to do.

'I finish off with a machine-gun shot,' he said. 'Unfortunately, I have not brought a machine gun with me.'

Voice from the back: 'That can *soon* be arranged.'

Terry Griffiths gives the problem some careful consideration.

BIZARRE
VENUES

If anyone thinks that the Cursed Hyperbole of Estate Agents is a new disease, here is proof that they were up to their tricks before the First World War. In 1912 a man rented a car and drove a considerable distance to view an 'old world' house also billed as having seven bedrooms, a dressing room and a billiard room.

He soon established that the old world must have ended rather recently in those parts, and that there were either six bedrooms and a dressing room or seven bedrooms and no dressing room. Still, there was nothing outrageously wrong with the place. He asked if he could see the billiard room.

The lady owner looked blank. 'Billiard room?' she asked.

The viewer showed her the agent's list. 'Hmm,' she said, still none the wiser. Then an idea dawned. 'I suppose they must mean the attic,' she said, and led the way to the top landing where there was a trap-door in the ceiling.

'It's up there,' said the lady. 'Would you like to go up? There's a ladder in the box-room that you can use.'

He declined. As he later said to a friend: 'You might conceivably have squeezed a half-sized bagatelle board through the trap-door. But nothing bigger or heavier. As for light, I don't think there was any.'

MOST WOBBLY

Inventors of the Edwardian period were much exercised with the problem of how to design a marine billiard table, i.e. one that could be installed on a ship and could be used in all weathers without the balls rolling all over the place every time the ship heaved, pitched or lurched in any way.

It was not a novel problem. I.K. Brunel's massive *Great Eastern*, conceived in the year of the Great Exhibition (1851) and launched with some difficulty six years later, had a billiard table on a swinging deck; but she did not last long as a passenger liner. In 1908 a grateful world was given the table which levelled itself mechanically. As the illustration shows, the bed remains level while all else around it is yawing about in time to the rhythms of the sea.

THE ILLUSTRATED LONDON NEWS

REGISTERED AT THE GENERAL POST OFFICE AS A NEWSPAPER.

No. 3636.— VOL. CXXXIII.   SATURDAY, DECEMBER 26, 1908.   SIXPENCE.

The Copyright of all the Editorial Matter, both Engravings and Letterpress, is Strictly Reserved in Great Britain, the Colonies, Europe, and the United States of America.

In the Billiard Room on the Great Eastern only the floor moves.

In 1911 a Mr W.G. Voonzaier, from what was then Cape Colony, was re-exploring the Brunel solution, claiming that he could design a billiard room for use at sea which would be so steady that players would have no sensation of being anywhere other than on *terra firma*. Has anyone heard what happened to him?

An outdoor tournament in the Dutch village of Moorn.

MOST GYROSCOPIC

After the ships, another transport oddity was the Brennan Mono-Rail, an experimental rail-car introduced in 1909. As *The Illustrated London News* explained:

'Each car is kept upright on the single rail by an adaptation of the gyroscope, two wheels revolving in opposite directions in a vacuum. This stability apparatus keeps the car in a stable condition no matter at what angle it may lie over.

'Now imagine a billiard table fixed in the car in such a way that it will be truly level when the car stands upright. A billiard ball placed on this table will, of course, lie still, the only force acting on it being that of gravity, acting vertically downwards. Suppose now that the car is running round a curve, and, consequently, lying over at an angle towards the inside of the curve. The table will lie over also; but the balls will remain stationary, as the centrifugal force acting on the balls and tending to throw them towards the outside of the curve is exactly counteracted by the upward slope of the table in that direction.

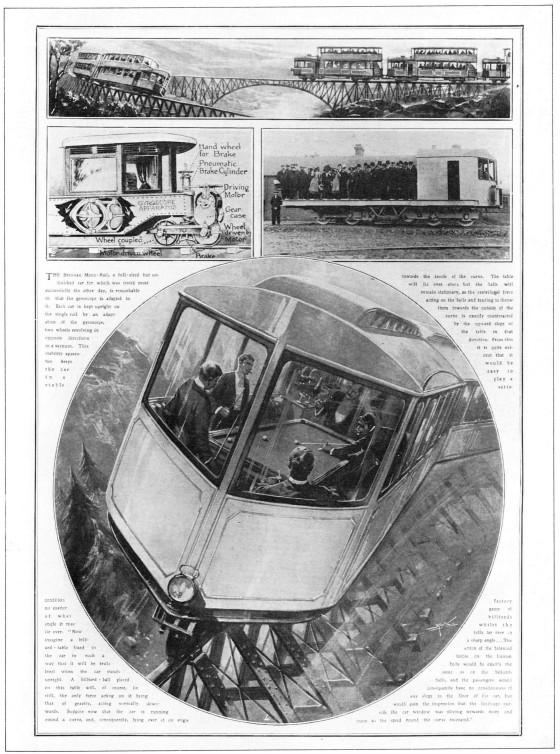

THE Brennan Mono-Rail, a full-sized but unfinished car for which was tested most successfully the other day, is remarkable in that the gyroscope is adapted to it. Each car is kept upright on the single rail by an adaptation of the gyroscope, two wheels revolving in opposite directions in a vacuum. This stability apparatus keeps the car in a stable condition no matter at what angle it may lie over. "Now imagine a billiard-table fixed in the car in such a way that it will be truly level when the car stands upright. A billiard-ball placed on this table will, of course, lie still, the only force acting on it being that of gravity, acting vertically downwards. Suppose now that the car is running round a curve, and, consequently, lying over at an angle towards the inside of the curve. The table will lie over also; but the balls will remain stationary, as the centrifugal force acting on the balls and tending to throw them towards the outside of the curve is exactly counteracted by the upward slope of the table in that direction. From this it is quite evident that it would be easy to play a satisfactory game of billiards whilst the table lay over at a sharp angle...The action of the balanced forces on the human body would be exactly the same as on the billiard-balls, and the passengers would consequently have no consciousness of any slope in the floor of the car, but would gain the impression that the landscape outside the car window was sloping upwards more and more as the speed round the curve increased."

Hand wheel for Brake
Pneumatic Brake Cylinder
Driving Motor
Gear-case
Wheel driven by Motor
GYROSCOPE APPARATUS
Wheel coupled to Motor-driven wheel
Brake

An artist's impression of the Brennan Mono-Rail.

'From this it is quite evident that it would be easy to play a satisfactory game of billiards whilst the table lay over at a sharp angle. The action of the balanced forces on the human body would be exactly the same as on the billiard balls, and the passengers would consequently have no consciousness of any slope in the floor of the car, but would gain the impression that the landscape outside the car window was sloping upwards more and more as the speed round the curve increased.'

Eh?

MOST NON-EXISTENT

Two professionals were booked to play at a club. They arrived in good time and were greeted by the manager. They asked to see the snooker room and were shown into a dining room. In the centre, a large space had been cleared.

'Right,' said one of the pros, nodding approval at the size of the room. 'Now where's the table?'

The manager looked at him as if he was mad. '*We* haven't got a table,' he said. 'Haven't you brought one with you?'

FIERCEST

In 1912, the manager of the billiards room at the Sydenham Palace Hotel, Coventry told *Billiards* magazine of the time, several years before, when he played 15-up on a miniature table at the King's Theatre, Gateshead. The table, by the way, was in the middle of a lion's cage in which two lions, under the watchful eye of their trainer, Miss Ella, were perched on stalls. The play was of a poor standard, and one of the lions frequently displayed his disgust.

QUEEREST-SHAPED

In 1946 – 47 Walter Donaldson trained for the next World Championship in almost total seclusion – in the converted loft of a bungalow in Belvedere, Kent. This extraordinary room was created by the owner, a Mr Brooke, who managed to get the full-sized table up there piece by piece. When it came to the slate bed, however, half the roof had to be removed.

For Donaldson, it turned out to be a happy training ground. In the final he beat Fred Davis 82 – 63.

BILLIARDS OUT OF DOORS

WE are indebted to Mr. Harold Holt of the George Street P

The chassis of a billiard table constructed for open-air games in the 1870s.

GRASSIEST

The Australian champion Walter Lindrum once compiled a break of 50 in 30 seconds on the lawn of a house in the Melbourne suburbs. The purpose of this feat was to prove Keith Miller, the Test cricketer, wrong after he had said that a player's skill in any sport depended on the playing surface to which he was accustomed; take away the familiar surface and the player would not be nearly as successful.

Lindrum challenged this statement, and a trial was set up on the lawn of the Melbourne house. A billiard 'table' was laid out, using six jam tins instead of pockets. To win, and also claim the $100 side-stake, Lindrum had to put together a half-century break in half a minute. He did so, and gave his winnings to a local charity.

MOST VENERABLE

Anyone going to play at Abertillery Central Club would suddenly find themselves faced with a very historic item: the old match table from the world-famous Leicester Square Hall. When the hall finally closed its doors in 1955, the table was brought by the *News Chronicle* which offered it as the prize in a five-a-side snooker tournament. Abertillery were the winners and off the table went to Wales.

WHAT
THE
VIEWERS
THINK

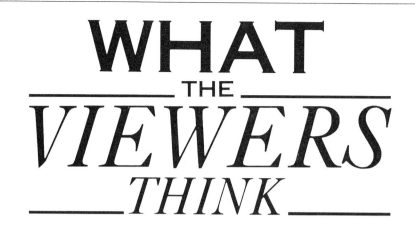

The viewers think… that Tony Knowles has quite a nice bottom. Not the best in town, but OK. He was voted third in a poll conducted in 1985 by BBC Television among staff and viewers. The others in, as they say, reverse order were:

Second: Jimmy White.

First: Kirk Stevens.

In a way this was retribution for Knowles, who excited a lot of comment the previous year when he told *The Sun* that he rated girls not out of ten, but out of two: those who say no, and those who say yes. This sparked a fashion for T-shirts bearing the legend: 'I SAID NO TO TONY KNOWLES'.

Tony Knowles seems to be looking with disbelief at Kirk Stevens, winner of the BBC poll.

This viewer thought... that the table being used for a televised tournament was the wrong size. He phoned the BBC to complain, and assured them that the table was square, not oblong. How could he tell? the BBC wanted to know.

'I've measured it on my telly,' he said.

This viewer thought... he could win a BBC competition. At the start of the 1984 World Championship, the BBC announced that they were going to have another 'Shot of the Championship' competition. As a way of demonstrating how the competition worked, they showed the three winning shots from the previous year.

This viewer did not quite get the right idea. He sent in his entry immediately, listing the three shots he had just seen. He still got them in the wrong order!

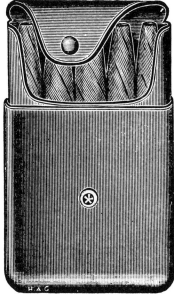

This viewer liked a flutter. In 1983 he travelled from Millwall to Preston, ignoring the comforts of hearth and telly. He took with him his life savings of £7,000 and invested the lot on Steve Davis, backing him at 4 – 6 to win the Coral UK Championship. Davis finished runner-up to Alex Higgins.

But what about Old Man Davis? Steve's father Bill usually gets through a normal-sized cigar per frame when he is watching Steve play. During the excruciatingly slow quarter-final in the 1985 World Championships between Cliff Thorburn and Dennis Taylor, the word is that he got through two eight-inch Churchill-thick cigars. And who can blame him.

This viewer thought... that the live audiences make far too much noise with their coughing and other disagreeable habits. On 1 February 1985, a Mrs S. Seacombe of Abingdon wrote to the *Daily Telegraph:* 'Sir, There must be a fortune to be made from selling cough lozenges to snooker audiences...'

Spectator noise had not been a problem when in 1982 Jim Meadowcroft played Bernard Bennett in the Professional Players Tournament in Birmingham. These two played before a paying audience of one – the lowest recorded attendance at a match involving two professionals in tournament play.

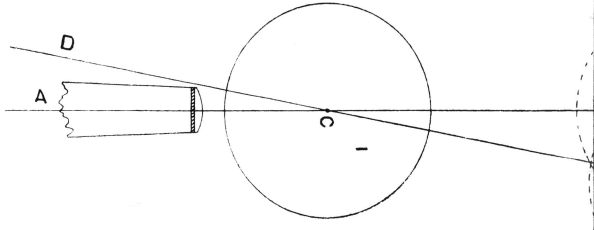

Quite what the viewers think... when Ted Lowe lets go one of his little asides is not recorded, but we suggest that life would not be the same without the man who once said of referee John Smyth, when he was taking a ball marker out of his pocket: 'John Smyth is getting his little implement out...'

And once described Bill Werbeniuk as 'Twenty stone of Canadian fat.' Not the most tactful remark at the best of times. Bill Werbeniuk was quite put out – he weighed only nineteen stone at the time!

Whatever the viewers think... they certainly love their snooker. If there is any doubt about that, a look at the viewing figures will prove the case. In 1985, 2.5 million watched the action on the quietest afternoon – and 18.5 million saw the final. Snooker, undoubtedly, is the most popular sport on television.

What do you think?

Ted Lowe (above) appears to be assessing Bill Werbeniuk (left) from all angles in an attempt to be more accurate next time.

119

ACKNOWLEDGMENTS

The Publishers would like to acknowledge with thanks
the following sources which supplied some of the
stories around which this book has been developed:

Everton's News Agency, Oddfax, Thurston & Co. Ltd.

The Publishers would also like to thank the following
sources for their help in providing illustrations:

BBC Hulton Picture Library
11, 12 top, 15, 27, 36, 40, 44, 48, 76 top and bottom, 79 top, 82 both, 92,
102, 104, 108 both.
Mary Evans Picture Library
12 bottom, 42, 43, 47, 64, 76 middle, 96, 101 both, 103
The Illustrated London News Picture Library
33, 67, 84, 100, 111, 113
David Muscroft
16, 19 both, 22 both, 24 both, 29 both, 32, 50, 51, 57, 60, 61, 68, 69, 70,
75, 85, 90, 91, 106, 107, 109, 116, 119 both
The Photo Source
23, 86, 88, 112
Syndication International
31, 62, 74, 81, 89